LEGACY OR PROPHECY?

• What are the strange revelations in the dimensions of the Great Pyramid? And is there a key to unlock its mysteries?

• Could a people whose culture was only one step removed from the Stone Age have actually designed and built such a monument?

• What accounts for the amazing powers and strange effects of a pyramid's shape on physical objects—what mysterious forces enable it to sharpen dull razor blades and preserve food for months?

• How is it possible that so many of man's sciences are embodied in the marvelous structure called the Great Pyramid—astronomy, mathematics, physics, optics, hydraulics, and even magic?

• Is this awe-inspiring monument conclusive evidence of a highly evolved civilization which flourished before recorded history?

• Is there truth to the stories of intensified mystical experiences that result from spending several hours alone in the main chamber?

THE GREAT PYRAMID:
Man's Monument to Man
by Tom Valentine

PINNACLE BOOKS • NEW YORK CITY

THE GREAT PYRAMID:
MAN'S MONUMENT TO MAN

Copyright © 1975 by Tom Valentine

An original Pinnacle Books edition, published for the first time anywhere.

ISBN: 0-523-00517-2

First printing, June 1975
Second printing, July 1975
Third printing, November 1975
Fourth printing, May 1976
Fifth printing, September 1976

Printed in the United States of America

PINNACLE BOOKS, INC.
275 Madison Avenue
New York, N. Y. 10016

THE GREAT PYRAMID:
MAN'S MONUMENT TO MAN

INTRODUCTION

The first time I stared at the rugged exterior of the Great Pyramid of Giza, the largest of man's accomplishments in stone, I was filled with awe at the enormity of the monument. At the same time I was appalled at its condition and the state of the immediate environment. The Great Pyramid, Man's Monument to Man, had been stripped of its original beauty and perfection. Now it was littered, vandalized, trampled, and urinated upon through ages of ignorance and apathy.

I had come to Egypt to explore and perhaps even worship in this ancient structure. My controversial theory and unorthodox thinking about the Great Pyramid would one day be a book. Was I about to encounter facts that would force a reconsideration? The visit to Giza convinced me beyond a doubt that our standard textbooks and the accepted legends of The Great Pyramid are all erroneous.

1

However, even as the academicians are wrong in saying this magnificent monument was built as a tomb for a Pharaoh, so too are the mystics and occultists wrong in many of their notions. The purpose of the Great Pyramid is very clear to me, and it is amazingly profound.

As I clambered over the huge stone blocks, ascending the pyramid, I shouted with joy, to the amazement of my Arab guide. Despite the vandalism and the centuries of erosion, the evidence of masonic perfection was obvious. The tremendous differences between the Great Pyramid and its neighbors on the plateau were obvious. Standing near the original entrance and studying the ancient stonework I recalled a story I had heard.

A modern contractor boasted of how modern methods and equipment could make the building of the Great Pyramid "child's play."

I wondered how a builder could possibly be accurate enough in his assessment of modern workmen and machines, and how they would go about placing the more than 2.3 million blocks of stone atop one another. In my mind's eye I tried to visualize an army of hardhats working with cranes and forklifts and trucks, perhaps even a railroad spur. Giant helicopters, even? I visualized the signal whistle and the pay line; the engineers and the union bosses.

No. No way. We don't have a construction firm today that could handle the job. Hell, we have trouble enough building a section of highway without numerous change orders, material delays, and reevaluation of cost estimates. Not to mention union restrictions.

I felt the limestone blocks and foolishly tried to count them. I stood at the base of each corner and noted that as much as 30 feet of masonry had been peeled off the original corners. It was easy to see why any theory based upon the exterior measurements was controversial. It would require geometry to develop any accuracy.

I even climbed to the top. That is against the rules, but a small bribe to an Arab guide and a start in the quiet early morning hours got around the problem. From the top the view is georgeous, spectacular.

Later, while exploring inside, I rushed to the huge blocks of granite that blocked the first ascending passage. The entry is forced around these blocks. One of the keys in the experts' argument is whether these three- or four-ton granite blocks could have been skidded down the 130 feet of narrow passage. Orthodox Egyptologists say that's what happened. Engineers, architects, and I contend it is not possible. I noted that less than a 16th of an inch of clearance existed all the way around the block. Not enough clearance to slide the blocks into place from above. My first-hand check agreed with my studies.

Although it is not a key issue in this book, there is a great deal of interest in the stories of mystical experiences enhanced by spending a few hours alone in the main chamber. Another bribe and I was allowed to spend the night inside the King's Chamber in silence. I spent only two hours in solitude, but it was enough to convince me that profound experiences indeed take place, but it depends upon one's definition of the mystical whether they are indeed such.

After catching my breath from the climb, it took me some time to come around to appreciate the situation. Alone at last! The huge granite sarcophagus, chipped and brutalized, captured my attention for a moment, then became my resting place. For several minutes my mind toyed with foolishness, and I tested the remarkable accoustics in the chamber. I think a group of musicians would do well to record in this chamber. Finally I settled down and savored the magnificent silence. I began to seriously contemplate my presence in this place of greats.

Then, as if guided by some unseen force, but most likely stemming from my own ultra-consciousness, I gave way to profound introspection. Why was I here? Why am I? What progress have I truly made in this lifetime toward my ultimate goals? Aspect by aspect, virtue by virtue, I opened myself to Me. There were no visible manifestations. I heard no voices inside my head, but I was aware of being far greater than the everyday me.

"Those who come here anticipating greater beings to manifest themselves, come here to satisfy prideful egos. True initiation begins with sincere self-appraisal," were the words focused upon in my mind. Perhaps it was only my own echoes. I only know that I put myself through the most honest introspection of my life, and though human perfection is very distant at this time, I came away from the experience with a renewed confidence that I have improved and am continuing to make progress.

Another issue is the matter of secret chambers and a passageway leading from the Sphinx to the

Great Pyramid. I had already written that no such chambers or passages exist and the Great Pyramid is monument enough without such frills. My guide, an aged Arab named Sam, told me how Europeans once urged the Egyptians to probe the Sphinx for secret chambers and the uphill slope of the Great Pyramid for an underground passage. The accommodating Egyptians drilled a number of small core holes into the solid rock Sphinx and into the plateau and found nothing. To those who believe the paws of the Sphinx harbor some secret chamber, I note that both have been rebuilt after being ripped asunder.

Unless a person has had the fortune to be taught history by one of those rare instructors who fears not to deviate from the textbook norm, he will have been taught that the Great Pyramid is merely the biggest of many such structures built by egomaniacal Pharaohs who sought immortality through entombment in these geometrical monuments. Even those few students who specialize in ancient Egyptian history get only a cursory review of the tallest building erected by man until the 20th century.

Generally speaking, we are taught that the Great Pyramid was the crowning achievement of the dynasties in ancient Egypt famed for building the massive tombs. We accept that a ruler, whose Greek name is given as Cheops and whose Egyptian name was Khufu, had the huge monument built as a home for his mummified remains. This idea is accepted on the basis of very sketchy evidences and the writings of Herodotus, a Greek journalist who has been acclaimed the "father of history."

We are taught many things in school, and why should we doubt what we are taught by our own institutions? I recall that my high school history instructor impressed me tremendously and I wanted to be a history major in college. The dogmatic overview of history I received in high school was so much a part of my thinking, that I remember being quite upset when Dr. Adolf Stone, my first college history professor, opened his initial lecture with: "We must always remember that history is precisely that—*his* story, and nothing more." Dr. Stone stressed how historians traditionally tend to color facts to suit their notions. Perhaps not intentionally all the time, but bias of one sort or another is generally present. Any king's chronicler, for example, would most likely bend over backward to make his employer look like a pretty good leader of men whether this was so or not.

Warped viewpoints of historic events often, over the years, become generally accepted fact and have a great influence on our thinking. Often the records unearthed by archeologists were originally falsified merely to establish ruling family dynasties. Scholars digging into the chronicles of ancient Egypt are familiar with the various listings of the kings and the falsifications found in some versions. I suspect the beginning of the First Book of Chronicles in the Old Testament, the part that lists all those names of who begat who for generation after generation, was designed by Ezra to give more political clout to the Levites.

The point of this is to make it perfectly clear

that what we are told by history isn't necessarily so. And archeology, the backbone for the study of the ancients, is at best a picture puzzle science with many pieces missing. Quite often the archeologists will establish a framework for their puzzle and will discard pieces that don't fit rather than rearrange the framework. This point has been clearly demonstrated by the sudden emergence of new theories of ancient history based mainly on pieces of the puzzle that obviously don't fit the standard framework. The popular concept of "ancient astronauts" is a leading example.

If one takes the time and effort to really study the Great Pyramid at Giza, the first conclusion must be that no people whose culture was only one step removed from the Stone Age could have possibly designed and built such a monument. In order to make the Great Pyramid fit the puzzle framework a number of terribly obscure assumptions were made by Egyptologists.

If you read any of the standard texts on the pyramid-building dynasties, you will note that whenever the Great Pyramid is discussed the material is prefaced with: "Although there are no records, it is assumed that . . ." It is also curious that this most remarkable of all man's monuments is usually granted only a few paragraphs while the other monuments, which no doubt were erected as tombs, are accorded entire chapters. The obvious difference is that while the Great Pyramid is the most fantastic, there is no basis in historic fact for a detailed discussion of it builders and its purpose. The others have writings inside, and paraphernalia of the period were found inside and

7

some records were unearthed that described the individuals responsible.

In my opinion, the erroneous assumption that the Great Pyramid of Giza was a tomb for Cheops and nothing more, plus the assumption that civilizations did not exist prior to Sumeria and Egypt, are the two grossest mistakes in all of man's recorded history. The generally accepted notion that mankind has no solid heritage beyond the digs of the ancient Middle East, and that civilizations before capable of evolving mankind toward perfection have not flourished, has retarded the overall consciousness that enhances character growth and harmony with the environment. Our history is essentially one war after another; gruesome tales of man's narrowness and inhumanity. For every brilliant flash of harmony and attainment, there are a dozen conflicts. Why? Could it be that our models, as presented by the accepted version of history, do not give us even a brief glimpse of man's ability to control himself and his environment in order to attain a perfect society? If we cannot conceive of a perfect society outside of the dreams of a few idealists, we cannot implant the idea of human perfection in our mass consciousness.

In this work, a part of man's past that displays perfection is laid out in terms easy for the layman to understand. It is my purpose to discuss every ramification of the Great Pyramid of Giza in an objective manner. The opening chapters deal with the structure's impressive size and precise construction. I debunk the tombic theory and attempt to supplant it with a thesis that withstands every assault of rationality. When all is said and done, much thought will have been provoked. Perhaps we will all have a greater sense of Man's purpose and potential when we consider the heritage of the Great Pyramid—Man's Monument to Man.

CHAPTER ONE

Wonder of Wonders

The ancient Greeks wrote into the annals of history that the Great Pyramid at Giza was the "first wonder of the ancient world." The genius of classical antiquity may have chosen more wisely than they themselves realized. Today there is controversy regarding the Great Pyramid's origin and purpose, with our standard textbooks insisting that it was nothing more than a tomb for a megalomanic Pharaoh named Cheops (or Khufu, as the Egyptians called him). There is no hard fact on which this tombic theory is based, and there is an avalanche of evidence to the contrary, but in the eyes of orthodoxy, a pyramid is a tomb, is a tomb, is a tomb. All the other pyramid-shaped monuments in Egypt were found to be tombs, so the Great Pyramid must also be a tomb. At this point, the controversy isn't important, so rather than stress what the Great Pyramid is not, let's review

11

some concrete, irrefutable facts about this wonder of wonders.

First of all there's no comparison between it and the others when it comes to size and precision of workmanship. The Great Pyramid is massive. If you visualize a forty-story building rising angularly from a 13½-acre base, you get a good idea of the size of the structure. It has been estimated that the huge cathedrals of Milan and Florence, St. Paul's Basilica in Rome, and Westminster Abbey could be set within the confines of the Great Pyramid's base. Were we to grind the stone in its structure into gravel, we could lay a roadbed eighteen feet wide and a foot thick all the way from New York to Salt Lake City. The length of one side of it's square base is more than two and a half football fields.

Each of the four triangular sides sloping upward from the base covers an area of nearly 5½ acres. The exterior above the ground is 22 acres of surface, and at one time this exterior glistened in the sun like a brilliant jewel. White Tura limestone casing stones, finely polished, reflected light from the sun and the moon as did no other object ever built by man. The core masonry is made up of an estimated 2,300,000 blocks of limestone hewn from nearby quarries. The smallest of these blocks weighs nearly three tons. These huge pieces of limestone were cut, roughly dressed, and fitted together with a precision unmatched in any other pyramid. The casing stones, quarried and transported across the Nile to the building site, were one hundred inches thick and weighed up to fifteen tons. These huge casings were fitted with an optician's precision. Some of these casings still in place are fitted so well that a business card cannot be inserted between the joints. The cement is so fine and amazingly strong that it boggles the minds of stonemasons today. The polished limestone blocks will fracture before the adhesion will give, although less than a fiftieth of an inch separates the blocks.

There is such a difference in the skill of the workmanship displayed between the Great Pyramid and the Second Pyramid that it is inconceivable that only one generation separated the two structures—a fact never mentioned in standard texts.

You should be getting the idea now. The Great Pyramid is big and well built. It is such a fantastic piece of work that it has caught the fancy of every thoughtful visitor for the past 5,000 years. More words of praise have been written about this monument than there are blocks of stone in its makeup.

Incidentally, you may see pictures of the Giza pyramid complex where the Second Pyramid of Cephren appears to be taller than Cheops. This is because the Second Pyramid is built on higher ground and still has an apex or capstone, while the apex of the Great Pyramid is missing. Some legends say the capstone of the Great Pyramid was made of pure gold and was therefore the first thing looted; others say it was a glistening crystal that sent energy out into space; and still others say it was highly polished granite. Since we are dealing with fact, we'll ignore these legends, but you can readily see how easily intrigue and mystery can surround this vast and perfect monument.

The vastness of the job is one of the unsolved mysteries still perplexing today's scholars. Most of the other mysteries are avoided by the learned academicians, but they do allow that they have no idea how people living in the culture we assume existed in Egypt at the time could have built such an edifice. For example, that the Egyptians cut the rough blocks of the core masonry with the bronze tools of the day is not inconceivable, but they had to hew out of the quarries more than one hundred blocks a day, seven days a week in order to finish the job in sixty-two years. Then, of course, the stones had to be transported to the building site and put into place. How they managed to cut and dress the hard rose-colored granite blocks, which are said to weigh more than eighty-five tons each, transport them more than 200 miles to the site, and put them in place is even harder to determine. Cheops, or Khufu, according to the best guesses of modern scholars such as Dr. I. E. S. Edwards, ruled for only twenty-three years. This means his workers, or slaves, had to design, cut, transport, and fit all the core blocks at a speed of 300 per day, seven days a week in order to get everything ready during their boss's reign.

The truth is, we don't know who, how, or when the Great Pyramid was built, despite the fact that scholars have a pretty good data bank regarding all the other pyramids, which were undoubtedly tombs. Even the most dogmatic and pompous of Egyptologists is forced to admit he has no idea how the ancients managed to construct the Great Pyramid. A number of theories have been advanced, ranging from slaves tugging the blocks with ropes (but where did they get all that rope?)

14

and rolling them on logs (and where did they get all those trees?) to the notion of mystics levitating the huge stones. Even if either of these two theories is correct, it is still not known how the masons applied the pressure required to dress the stones. It has been estimated that 2,000 pounds of pressure per square inch is needed to do the dressing work on the granite blocks. One student of the Great Pyramid has suggested that the greatest loss to modern times has been the apparent ability these ancient builders had to gather and organize such a work force.

Pyramids in general and the Great Pyramid in particular are far more ancient than the other images conjured up by thoughts of historic Egypt. The Great Pyramid existed thousands of years earlier than Ikhnaton and Nefertiti, than Moses and the Exodus, than Antony and Cleopatra. In fact, it is because the Great Pyramid is so far removed from us in time that we have only elusive theories to work with. Estimates of when the structure was completed range from as far back as 73,000 years ago when "the lyre was in Taurus," to the generally accepted estimate of when Cheops lived, about 2600 B.C. It is curious that among all the pieces of evidence archeologists have uncovered that offer clues to the life and times of Cheops, nothing has been unearthed that conclusively links him with the construction of the Great Pyramid. There is a reference to Cheops having made some repairs, which seems to indicate that the building had been around for some time to need a little patch-up work. A lot of the speculation hinges on a painted cartouche found on the unpolished sides of the huge granite blocks

15

that make up the ceiling of the main chamber of the Great Pyramid's interior. A cartouche on an Egyptian monument is an oval or oblong figure containing the name of a ruler or a deity, and since the Pharaohs were considered to be gods, their names were in cartouches. The particular cartouche found on the granite of the Great Pyramid is said to prove Khufu built the structure. However, what the scholars are not telling is that the name "Khufu" is awfully close to the word "Khuti," and both mean "Glorious Light" or "Horizon of Heaven," depending on the interpreter. This word "Khuti" happens to be the word for "pyramid," and this could very well mean that the Pharaoh took his name from the grand, glistening structure that overlooked his kingdom, rather than the other way around. It is generally believed by Egyptologists that a pyramid worship cult built up around Khufu and lasted for about 400 years. Since it is not likely that the Great Pyramid could have been constructed during the 23-year reign of the Pharaoh, it is much more reasonable to assume that he developed the cult by adopting the mysterious and beautiful monument of polished stone that had already been standing on the plateau for about a thousand years. The smaller mastabas and temple surrounding the Great Pyramid, which are conclusively linked to Khufu's period, would indicate such an adoption process. This is my theory, and it holds to logic more tenaciously than the currently accepted theory. At least the adoption thesis is not forced to account for how the Egyptians erected the huge structure during the twenty-three years of Khufu's reign, using the tools and know-how we attribute to that period in Egyptian history. One thing is certain amid all the guesswork—the Great Pyramid has been dominating the landscape for a long, long time, and it has outlasted everything else of importance in the ancient world. Where, for example, are the Hanging Gardens of Babylon, the Colossus of Rhodes, the Lighthouse at Alexandria, and the fantastic city of Troy?

To heighten the mystery, we find that not only is the Great Pyramid distinctly superior in size, shape, and excellence of workmanship, but also in orientation, location, and geometric precision.

The orientation of the Great Pyramid to the cardinal points of the compass doesn't interest many people, but that's only because people seldom stop to ponder the difficulty of locating true north while living on a sphere that is spinning through the great void of space. We take the directions for granted these days, but 99.9 percent of us would fail dismally if we were required to locate true north using only the devices we ascribe to the ancient Egyptians. The near perfect orientation of the Great Pyramid has caused great scholars to shake their heads in disbelief. How did the builders of this monument determine true north? After all, they are said to be only one step removed from the Stone Age—a period when ape-like creatures carried clubs, lived in caves, and hauled their women around by the hair. Frankly, the generally accepted view of prehistory is a gross distortion, and our ideas of the past need serious revision.

Recently the Great Pyramid's remarkable orientation became a matter of scientific speculation once again. The March 1973 issue of *Science* magazine pictured the Giza complex on the cover and featured an article by two foreign researchers who stated that the Great Pyramid is twisted slightly to the left, or off true north by about four minutes of arc. The researchers reason that the original structure was perfectly oriented, so the slight misalignment indicates either a shift in the earth's pole or a movement of the African continent. Now that's pretty heady stuff. Some unknown ancient builders, living just a few generations after the Stone Age, laid out this huge, square-based monument so precisely that modern-day scientists will seriously consider that the continent shifted rather than that the workmen were inaccurate and built it with a twist to the left.

Since the Second and Third Pyramids are also twisted slightly, I am curious to know why these researchers have not considered earthquake and subsidence effecting the entire plateau in a similar manner. Regardless of the problem, it's obvious that the orientation of the Great Pyramid is impressive. It is said that when famed Renaissance astronomer Tycho Brahe set out to orient his observatory at Urambourg to true north, he missed by eight minutes of arc—or about twice what the Great Pyramid misses on its east side—due perhaps to something other than the builder's aligning ability.

Today we have gyroscopes and electronic gear and orbiting satellites, and we know pretty well which way is up, or north, but we are at least 5,000 years smarter than the pyramid builders. The inconsistency of it all is appalling. If the general notion about the ancient Egyptians is correct and they had a Bronze Age culture incapable of higher mathematics (we like to credit the Greeks of classical times with inventing math), they viewed their world as flat and somewhat smaller than the planet earth. They supposedly didn't know such a thing as a pole existed, so they couldn't have cared about true north. If that's true, then the orientation to the poles is a coincidence—and so are the location and the geometric precision.

Not only did they accidentally orient the Great Pyramid to the cardinal points, but they accidentally selected the prime meridian and the tropic of Capricorn as a location. Pick up a globe map of the earth, and use a piece of string to make the meridian (line from north pole to south pole) through the spot where the Great Pyramid is located. You will notice that you cross the greatest mass of land on the planet's north-south axis. If you are going to attempt to disprove this, please be certain to subtract the difference from large bodies of water whenever alternate meridians are considered. The Pyramid meridian misses the extended tip of Africa—but not northern Europe!

Such a meridian would be perfect for use as the earth's prime meridian. It makes more sense than using the line that passes through Greenwich, England.

The line going around the globe from west to east, or the Pyramid's precise latitude, also appears to pass through more land mass than any other line. There are many people who believe that the Great Pyramid is therefore situated at the center of the earth's land mass and exactly quarters that mass. It's either a happy coincidence or planned that way, and if it was planned, somebody knew a lot more about the size and shape of our planet than we give the Egyptians credit for knowing at that time. As we go along, it will become more and more apparent to you that whoever built the Great Pyramid knew as much or more about this planet than we know today.

In answer to anyone who claims the orientation was coincidence because the early Egyptians could not possibly have known our planet is a sphere that orbits the sun, I'd like to take this opportunity to point out that one of Pharaoh's many glorious titles was "Lord of the Orbit." Now, I ask you—orbit of what?

Finally we find that the Great Pyramid is also distinctly superior in regard to geometric precision. Long before Pythagoras, some pyramid designer knew about the 3-4-5 triangle and the 2-square root of the 5-3 triangle. Long before Archimedes traveled to Egypt and then returned to Syracuse and exclaimed, "Eureka" (meaning, "I found it"), some pyramid designer was aware of the universal geometric relationship between the diameter of a circle and its circumference (3.14159). Even the mathematical concept of pi, or the "Golden Mean," was evidently known by the designer of the Great Pyramid.

As we shall see later, certain rugged individuals refused to ignore many pieces of the Great Pyramid's evidential puzzle, therefore many "outlandish" theories based on the structure's geometric precision have developed. So many unusual and utterly fantastic things are implied by the linear measurements and slopes of angle that the Great Pyramid has been surveyed more closely than any other edifice ever erected. Before any more is said, we must realize that all the measurements have been taken in modern times, many thousands of years after construction. Earthquakes, subsidence, wind and sand erosion, human vandalism, and perhaps even continental drift have wended by since the days of the Pyramid's construction. Despite this, the perfections implied in the structure of the Great Pyramid are mind-boggling. Such perfections incorporated into a pyramid shape could not have been discovered by studying the Second or Third or any other pyramids—they simply don't have it. The other two large pyramids at Giza are grand attempts at copying a forgotten ability that had been known by a culture antedating these Egyptians. The Egyptians were remarkable enough in their own right, but their work attests to their having too little too late.

The prime question regarding the Great Pyramid, no matter what theory one favors, is why was it built at all? Why would any people go to the Herculean effort to build a monument the likes of the Great Pyramid? The implications are awesome. To avoid confronting more serious and far-reaching possibilities, scholars cling tenaciously to the idea that it was nothing more than a tomb for a ruling maniac. A tomb certainly didn't require the various aspects of material and geometric perfection embodied in this grandest of monuments. This inference is made all the more obvious when we see that all the other pyramids, which were tombs, didn't have material and geometric precision. From the evidence unearthed, scholars cannot determine who, how, or when the Great Pyramid was built. Perhaps archeological proof will never be found to solve those mysteries.

However, does it really matter? Must we know the names of the obviously super-intelligent builders, and must we understand their methods of construction, and must we know the exact dates of the construction to understand that this monument has a great deal of significance? I don't think so. If the "why" of the Great Pyramid can be shown with reason, and we can make use of what is implied, then the rest is superfluous information.

Before we tackle the "why" in detail, let's first explore an outline of history that disagrees with the accepted view of what went on many thousands of years ago, but does indeed agree with much archeological evidence that has been heretofore ignored and left outside the framework of historical understanding.

CHAPTER TWO

A Remnant of Prehistoric Civilization

I am convinced the builders of the Great Pyramid were a remnant of a fantastic civilization that existed during the ages we now call "prehistoric." Anyone who gives any serious thought to *how* some ancient Middle Eastern cultures developed certain bodies of knowledge will consider it obvious that these cultures *inherited* a vast amount of data from some sort of culture that existed in the dim past. For example, the complexities of gravitational astronomy were known by the Great Pyramid builders, and accurate interpretations from the complex study of astrology were made by the Chaldeans. Both of these bodies of knowledge require thousands of years to verify and both require complicated mathematics. We are asked to believe that some time between 5000 B.C. and 3000 B.C. people stepped out of the Stone Age and into the Bronze Age with knowledge of the earth's orbit around the sun, the planet's size and shape, and the fact that our planet wobbles as it revolves—knowledge handed down to them from observations made by shepherds who watched the stars. Discovering that there is a difference between planets and stars while lolling around on the desert and peering into the heavens is a good trick in itself. Try watching the stars for a few nights yourself; then figure out how many years it would take for you to determine that because the sphere we reside on wobbles as it revolves, there appears to be a slightly different positioning of the stars each year, and that this precessional cycle takes almost 26,000 years to complete. After a couple of observations, you're likely to toss your hands up and say, "Who cares?" Somebody had to care, or else we could not afford the luxury of taking our calendar and present-day space flights for granted.

It's also apparent to anyone who doesn't require that the history of mankind on our planet fit into the mold shaped by present-day academics that the Mayans of the Western half of the world also acquired knowledge of gravitational astronomy from somewhere and were thus able to produce a precise calendar.

The body of knowledge required to understand precession and its relation to the ecliptic (path of the earth's orbit around the sun) was handed down from somewhere—the problem is, from where?

Erich Von Daniken, whose book *Chariots of the Gods* was a best-seller and inspired a television special, would have us believe that the only logical

24

answer is that highly intelligent creatures from outer space landed on this planet and brought their knowledge with them. This thesis, which gets us even more excited each time newspapers carry stories of UFO sightings, cannot be disproved—but I don't accept it.

There are many things that make up the acceptance of a theory, a notion or a belief, and one of them is intuition. Intuition is a quality of mind we all have, and all of us use it more often than we may be aware. My intuition rejected Von Daniken's thesis just as it rejected the standard textbook version of history. In addition to simply feeling that something is wrong, I find that both the gods from outer space theory and the theory that history only began about 5,000 years ago are vulnerable to attacks of rationality.

I agree with Von Daniken's thinking that the evidence shows man may have traveled into space during one of his ancient civilizations. However, the ability to soar beyond this planet's atmosphere does not need to be introduced by beings from another world. Mankind could well have developed the know-how, then lost it in cataclysmic change, leaving the survivors of the cataclysm only memories of the glorious past to carve into rocks and to otherwise slowly distort the previously known facts into legend to the confusion of future archeologists.

Perhaps the best argument against Von Daniken's thesis comes from stone carvings that he emphatically points to as evidence that our forefathers may have arrived here from Venus. In South America a huge stone gate has carved on it an apparent reference to the orbit of Venus and the Venusian calendar of 225 days. Since Venus makes only six revolutions in its orbit around the sun, a Venusian would naturally describe his calendar as having six very long days. However, if an earth person observes Venus, the time of the orbit will be 225, twenty-four-hour days. I therefore suggest the carving indicates clearly that someone had an accurate knowledge of another planet's orbit (but not revolutions) and noted the observations in earth-oriented terms.

The very first thing that occurs to me when I think about this matter is that somebody certainly had a lot of leisure time on his hands. There must have been an excellent educational system in those days.

In archeology it is easy to make an erroneous assumption. After all, the science of archeology is at best a jigsaw-puzzle science, and making deductions about a people and its culture from musty artifacts can be difficult when all the evidence must fit into a preconceived framework. I often wonder what the scholar of the distant future would deduce about us if he dug up the huge corten steel monstrosity that artist Pablo Picasso gave as a gift to the city of Chicago.

Seriously though, let's consider one of the major problems confronting archeology: the coexistence of cultures. For example, our twentieth-century world with its sophisticated technologies coexists with far simpler peoples, such as the Amish of the Midwest, the aboriginal tribes of Australia, and the Tasaday people of the Philippines. Could not some fantastic civilization have existed on land now covered by oceans, and have coexisted with Neanderthal and Cro-Magnon cultures that are considered on a par with the primitive tribes of Australia, South America, and the Philippines today?

To account for the builders of the Great Pyramid, and much other evidence, I accept the outline of history as presented in *The Ultimate Frontier* by Eklal Kueshana. It was in reading this remarkable book that I first became aware of the potentials of the Great Pyramid. Here is a brief summation of man's history as presented in *The Ultimate Frontier*.

After the Edenic state was brought to a close, man's first civilization began on a huge continent that is now almost entirely submerged beneath the Pacific Ocean. The dawning of this first civilization took place about 78,000 years ago, and though the people did not strive to attain the technological heights we have reached in modern times, they far surpassed us in the ability of society to help citizens generate purpose, peace, prosperity, and character growth. Some time prior to the time this civilization, often called Lemuria, was destroyed by a cataclysmic shift in the earth's crust, migrants developed a civilization on a group of large islands that are now beneath the Atlantic Ocean. This was the beginning of the "legendary" civilization of Atlantis. Other major civilizations also developed. One of them was called Osiris and existed in what is now the floor of the Mediterranean Sea, and the other was called Rama and existed in India. These later civilizations, especially Atlantis, developed a sophisticated technology with equipment that would amaze us today.

The continent of Mu in the Pacific was destroyed by a major cataclysm about 26,000 years

27

ago. The sinking of the huge land mass lowered the world's water level considerably and joined the islands of the Poseid Archipelago into a continent situated in the present-day Atlantic. This continent was itself submerged in two minor cataclysms and disappeared beneath the ocean about 11,000 years ago.

Now, the immediate question raised is: If these fantastic civilizations truly existed, where is the evidence? The bulk of the archeological evidences lies buried beneath oceans, seas of lava, rocks, and mud. A cataclysm is a violent physical change in the earth's surface, involving sudden upheaval, inundation, and volcanic activity. There is no doubt that the earth has undergone such cataclysmic changes in the past. The science of paleomagnetics (study of fossil magnetic records in rock formations) shows conclusively that land masses have shifted from one point to another in relation to the poles. The polar regions themselves have been located in various spots during the past 100,000 years. The Sudan Basin, the Caspian Sea, and the Laurentian Basin of Eastern Canada are all huge depressions in the earth's surface, depressions made by the sheer weight of ice—such as the permanent ice now depressing the Antarctic continent. There are some scientists today who estimate we may be due for another cataclysmic change relatively soon. Many people believe the Biblical prophecy of "Doomsday" is literally a prophecy of such a shifting of land masses.

Sea water rushing over a mass of shifting, submerging land would certainly have the required force to wipe out all evidences of civilization, even a civilization with all the steel and concrete we've poured over ours. Think of it this way: a garden hose with mild pressure built up by placing your thumb over part of the nozzle will knock dinnerware and other paraphernalia from a table top; a fire hose will knock men head over heels, so imagine what a tsunami will do. Tsunami is the Japanese word for a destructive force caused by a shock wave traveling through water. Earthquakes set up shock waves that travel at the speed of sound. When these shock waves travel in water, the speed is slowed slightly as water is pushed along by the activity. A tsunami travels at speeds in excess of 500 miles per hour. It has been predicted by both scientists and seers that the West Coast of the United States will be seriously damaged by a tsunami caused by earthquakes in the Orient. The tsunami action caused by the Anchorage, Alaska, earthquake damaged the harbor town of Crescent City, California, and in my hometown of Morro Bay an old friend lost his life in the sudden rise and fall of water as he stood on a floating dock.

During a cataclysm, shock waves and water are not alone in doing severe damage. Volcanic eruptions can cover huge areas with molten lava. The entire Pacific Northwest is buried beneath a massive lava flow. Huge tracts of land can be swallowed, and mountain ranges can be thrust upward in an instant when continental plates collide during a cataclysm. The force of such a collision is awesome. The oft-repeated story of the Bereskova mammoth is perhaps our best example of what can happen to life in a cataclysm. On the banks of the Bereskova River in Siberia, a woolly mammoth was found quick-frozen in the tundra. Some great force had smashed this huge mammal into the earth and refrigerated it so rapidly that the meat was still edible after thousands of years. The stunning blow caught the mammoth while it grazed quietly on grasses that grow in a temperate climate, nothing at all like the frozen Siberian countryside. This is a clear indication of a continental shift from one climate to another.

A cataclysm would leave only huddled groups of survivors. Those who did not go insane would be immediately relegated to a Stone Age existence, battling the elements for survival. Before long the wonders of a technological civilization would become dim memories to be handed down in the form of stories from parent to child.

To realize the plausibility of such a catastrophe, one merely needs to study the makeup of the earth's crust. Relatively speaking, the crust of this planet is as thin as an eggshell. The dozen tectonic or continental plates that make up the crust float on a bed of magma, which is a hot, plastic substance that flows as molten lava when the pressure is released. The plates are held in place on the slippery magma by forces inherent in the earth's axial spin. All that's needed to cause a sudden and drastic change in the positions of the plates is for something to break the delicate balance. It is believed by some, including myself, that the weight of the permanent ice at the South polar region is causing an imbalance that affects the axial spin. The ice pack is growing steadily, and by the turn of the century more than 98 percent of the earth's permanent ice will be weighing heavily on the Antarctic continent. This burden working in conjunction with other forces could trigger the continental shift.

Even though most of the evidence of previous civilizations was swallowed by cataclysm, there is an outstanding amount of evidence that such civilizations indeed existed, and those modern scholars who dogmatically deny this notion are fools. In the Pacific Islands alone there is enough evidence of previous civilizations to obliterate the theory that the cradle of civilization was the Middle East.

Geologically speaking, the continent of Mu, or Lemuria, is clearly outlined. The tectonic plate of Mu from North America, South America, and Asia encircles the vast area that includes all of Australia, New Zealand, the Philippines, Oceania, and part of North America. That California and Australia are part of the same continent seems borne out by the matching of soils and flora. The eucalyptus and acacia are native only to Australia and California. The story that the eucalyptus trees were imported from Australia to California is widely circulated, and it is true of some of the species—especially those grown for use as power poles. However, there are eucalyptus trees found along the central coast that are hundreds of years old and are definitely indigenous.

Within the ring of fire, the islands of Oceania are dotted with the ruins of some ancient and generally unexplained culture. These stone ruins of the Lemurian civilization were obviously not built by the island peoples living there today. On Ponape, one of the Caroline Islands, there are ruins of a city that could conceivably have housed more than a million inhabitants. Today there are less than 50,000 inhabitants on all of the Carolines.

It is pointed out in *The Ultimate Frontier* that this ancient city is called Metalanim, and the ruins indicate it was built of gigantic stone blocks weighing up to fifteen tons apiece. The stone used is not found on the islands today. Referring to Metalanim, *The Ultimate Frontier* says: "Artificial waterways capable of passing a modern battleship intersect the city. Metalanim is remarkable for its architectural and engineering excellence and is not at all like the primitive works one associates with the natives of Oceania. . . . This city was apparently built by the people of Lemuria of rock hewn from now submerged lands."

Illustrating clearly that Metalanim is not merely an isolated archeological mystery, there are remnants of forty stone temples of similar architectural design located on barren Malden Island some 3,000 miles from Ponape. Roadways of basalt blocks lead off in every direction from the temples and vanish into the Pacific. Ruins of the same type of roadway can be found on almost all of the islands of Oceania that are located within the ring of fire.

In addition, the famed ruins of Tiahuanaco on the shores of Lake Titicaca in Peru are similar in architectural and stone work to those of Metalanim. Tiahuanaco was once a seaport city, but today it is high in the Andes, a range of mountains that are generally regarded as having been formed in the present geological epoch and are part of the ring of fire.

To wrap up the evidence indicating a remote

civilization in the Pacific, *The Ultimate Frontier* states:

> Excavations south of Mexico City revealed a former ocean port which is now far inland at an elevation of 7,000 feet. When this ancient buried city was unearthed by William Niven, it had a total of thirty-one feet of debris above it consisting almost entirely of boulders, gravel and sand. The only way so much material of this type could have been deposited is by a tidal wave of colossal magnitude. If nothing else, these archeological findings indicate that man was well civilized during the last era of mountain-raising havoc and that he experienced floods of appalling destructiveness. The tale about Noah's Ark finds its inspiration in this event.

Following the destruction of Mu and the civilization that had existed there for 52,000 years without interruption, the culture of Atlantis flourished. The Atlantean civilization lasted for 14,000 years until its submersion about 9,500 B.C. Considering what we in America have accomplished during 200 years of conflict, turmoil, and squabbling, can you imagine the quality of a civilization lasting 14,000 years, as Atlantis did? I'm told we cannot imagine the fine quality of the Lemurian civilization that developed over 52,000 years. I have also been told, and I accept it as true though I cannot prove it, that it was a remnant of civilization from Mu continuing on through Atlantis that built the Great Pyramid and provided the inspiration for the Bible of Moses.

Because I refuse to make statements without offering support for them, we'll explore the evidence that a major civilization did exist in the Atlantic and that before it vanished in a cataclysm, much of its culture diffused to peoples on both sides of the ocean. Many books have been written that deal with the impressive array of evidence for the influence of a very real Atlantean culture, but we will only touch on a few items here.

There are only two direct references to Atlantis in literature; the famed "Timaeus" dialogue of Plato and the Bhagravad Purana from the Hindu culture. There's no way to guess how many direct references may have gone up in smoke when the library at Alexandria was put to the torch. The modern world also lost a golden opportunity for historic knowledge when the Bishop of Yucatan, Father DeLanda, ordered all the Mayan literature destroyed.

Plato's account is presented in his usual format. He created dialogues between characters to give his writing more life and readability. This is a technique that in no way detracts from the veracity of what he had to say. The dialogue, which takes place between Timaeus, Critias, Hermocrates, and Socrates, discusses the former civilization of Atlantis with extraordinary precision. Why scholars today should regard this dialogue as myth while not regarding Plato's other writings as such is beyond me. Plato simply wasn't the kind of person who diddled around with nonsense. The Atlantean story was not investigated by students of later periods because of the dictates of Aristotle, Plato's prize pupil. Aristotle, you may recall, was considered infallible by the dogmatic medieval church and his opinions were rigidly guarded as fact. Aristotle was the only classical Greek who considered Plato's account of Atlantis to be fiction.

There's a touch of irony here. Not only did Aristotle's opinion of Atlantis have a retarding effect on the study of history, but his views on astronomy (the earth is the center of the universe) and biology (spontaneous generation) became a later dogma and retarded science a thousand years. We are still clinging to his erroneous opinion of the Atlantis matter. Incidentally, Aristotle was one of the few famous Greek scholars who did not spend time studying in Egypt.

Anyway, Plato told of Solon's visit to the city of Sais, where he spoke with the Egyptian priests. Solon was told that "you Hellenes have no heritage," because cataclysms came along and wiped heritages out. The precise translation reads: "certain perturbations in the movement of heavenly bodies occur periodically causing the destructions." The priests then described the Atlantean empire, saying the upheaval ruined it about 9,000 years before Solon's time, or about 10,000 years before Christ. Actually, Plato's descriptions of Atlantis are far more believable than Herodotus' descriptions of how the Great Pyramid was built. There is further confirmation in the writings of Proclus, who tells how a Greek named Krantor journeyed to Sais, and priests in that Egyptian city showed him inscriptions in a temple relating essentially the same information told Solon and repeated by Plato.

Although Herodotus scoffed at the Egyptian claims to ancestral origin from a land "beyond the pillars of Hercules," he wrote it down. Archeologists digging in Egypt in the nineteenth century dug up a papyrus dating from the Second

Dynasty or about 3000 B.C. that tells of an expedition sent west into the Atlantic to search for the land of the ancestors.

It's curious that all of these references to "beyond" the Pillars of Hercules are conveniently ignored by anthropologists and archeologists who have worked so hard to build a case for the island of Santorini having been Plato's Atlantis. They have uncovered a lot of evidence that a great civilization did exist in the Osiri Valley, which is now the Mediterranean Sea.

Students of anthropology are taught that culture usually diffuses out from a center to affect peoples in various ways. For example, the Romans enjoyed chariot racing, and this sport diffused out from the center of the Roman Empire to many parts of the world. A cultural trait is a difficult thing to instill in people and it usually takes generations. Therefore it is far more likely that pyramid building, a trait of relatively advanced civilizations on both sides of the Atlantic, was diffused from a central culture. Other traits that require generations of tradition to build up are also found on both sides of the Atlantic, thus pointing to a central culture now beneath the sea. These include the mummification of human bodies, certain kinds of ceremonial tattooing, linguistic similarities, architectural similarities, and witchcraft.

Yes, even witchcraft. In a cave in Spain, ancient paintings depict female figures wearing pointed hats dancing around a phallus. Across the Atlantic we find that Tlasolteotl, the Aztec witch queen, wore a similar hat and rode a broomstick!

Another isolated trait occurring on both sides

36

of the Atlantic Ocean was city planning. Plato's description of the sacred or capital city of Atlantis was specific and detailed: "Citadel on a lofty eminence; ring upon ring of defending walls and alternate zones of land and water covered by arched bridges for ships to pass. Canals to the sea. . . ."

When Paul Auchler reconstructed the ancient city of Carthage, he found it identical to this description by Plato. There was a citadel on a hill, defending walls and alternating courses of land and water with canals and bridges, and finally a masked entrance to the sea. On the other side of the Atlantic, the city of Tenochtitlán, an ancient ruin where Mexico City stands today, there was a central pyramid or citadel on a hill, and water and land zones alternating with bridges and canals.

The evidence of a highly civilized prehistory is irrefutable if viewed with an open mind to such a likelihood. Since the evidence cannot be refuted, it is ignored.

The point of all this is to show that a long time ago, after cataclysms had destroyed the majority of their civilizations, the remnants of survivors who retained the knowledge of the vanished lands set out to accomplish an all-important task.

And now we must veer from physical matters to the nebulous area of man's spiritual nature in order to get a proper perspective of the Great Pyramid and its magnificent purpose. This is information for which I can offer no hard evidence, so it should be treated appropriately—consider it, and if it strikes you as valid, use it; if not, discard it. The purpose and significance of the Great Pyramid can be enhanced by acceptance of this information, but it won't be compromised by disregarding this part of the story—as you will see.

The purpose of civilization is to enhance each citizen's opportunity for Egoic, or character, growth. The purpose of life is to evolve ourselves from clods to God—to learn to use our minds fully and to attain human perfection, so we may move up the rungs toward our Creator. A civilization that does not enhance every citizen's chances by providing a sound economy, excellent education, and the tools for character development is not doing its job. Every individual has free will, and it is a law of the universe that one does not interfere in the environment or affairs of another without being asked to do so. By this combination of free will and ignorance of purpose, we have evolved a pretty sorry state of civilization over the past 11,000 years. However, our technology is adequate, and a great number of people feel intuitively that there is a better world to be made—so all is not lost. I believe we have been helped along the way by those individuals who evolved Egoically in the past great civilizations, and though they do not take us by the hand and do our work for us, they are ever present and striving to show us paths to excellence.

Evil is a very real thing. It was created by the combination of free will and ignorance, and it has been one of man's major contributions to civilization over the past 20,000 years. The battle between good and evil goes on whether we believe in it or not. Even today there is a battle for control of civilization between the forces of evil and the forces of the highest good for all concerned. The

Great Pyramid is a key factor in this struggle to help mankind help itself.

When it became obvious that humankind would succumb to the temptations of evil—the seeking of power and dominion over others, which is total interference in another's life—a body of evolved, wise men was formed to do what it could to help the unevolved Egos of the future. A Great Plan was laid out—a plan that would help men evolve from a Stone Age culture following the ruin of the past civilizations, to a magnificent civilization that is often called the Kingdom, or Nation of God. The times in which we live, you and I, are nearing the times of this great civilization where everyone strives for the highest good of everyone else. It may not look that way now, especially if you view our present society with a cynical eye. But there are millions of people alive today who are sincerely seeking a better way, who know in their hearts that this better way is dawning. America is far from perfect as societies go, but in the last 200 years we have made fantastic strides in the right direction, and America is an excellent stepping stone to that great civilization of the future.

This is the essence of the philosophy behind the hard evidence to be presented regarding the Great Pyramid—Man's Monument to Man.

CHAPTER THREE

Ancient Civilization Builders

Our history texts refer to them as Hyksos, the so-called Shepherd Kings. These people are said to have mysteriously entered the land of ancient Egypt on at least two distinct occasions in recorded times. They infiltrated and took over much of the governmental control without violence, made some social changes, then mysteriously vanished as if swallowed by the sands of the desert as well as the sands of time. There is mild controversy here, too. Some modern scholars, not content with assuming that a migratory group of people with unusual charisma could have slowly worked their way into power without warfare, have arbitrarily decided that the word "Hyksos" doesn't mean "Shepherd Kings," but rather interprete it to mean "rulers of foreign countries." Today's textbooks emphasize that the Hyksos invaded Egypt following a series of weak dynasties and were "probably Semitic people." The texts claim the Hyksos had the advantage of "horse-drawn chariots." It is apparent these Hyksos wandered over most of the Middle East and had a profound effect on the various kingdoms of the era. It is also apparent these ethnic "invasions" were without the necessary violence to be recorded as conflict, and that these tribal movements took place in migratory waves during known historic times. For our purposes here, let's assume that the Hyksos were in reality a small tribal group capable of impressing others with their life-style and abilities. To illustrate my thesis on how the Great Pyramid was erected long before Egypt became a powerful political unit, and how archeologists could be confused by the findings, I will outline what may have happened about 4,800 years before Christ.

The various tribal groups who inhabited the Nile delta for the thousands of years between the cataclysm that destroyed Atlantis and Osiris and the time of the first appearance of Hyksos were descendants of the flood's few hardy survivors, who eventually settled in this fertile location. These people were farmers who tilled the soil and managed to support livestock well enough to have a relatively civilized society. Not much progress had been made during the period of more than 5,000 years between the days of struggle after the floods and the days when a small tribal group of exceptionally talented and intelligent people arrived in the Northern Nile valley. At first the various village chiefs called their people to arms, since fighting strangers off the fertile farmlands was one of the hazards of the era. However, these newcomers were people of good will and good humor. They had no intention of fighting or trying to take something that belonged to others.

This group of wanderers had lived for centuries in what is now Ethiopia. The tribesmen were exceptional masons and artisans, and wherever they lived for any amount of time, they seemed to improve the conditions of the environment and peoples they encountered. They affected others unobtrusively, teaching more by example than by verb. Whenever others showed a keen interest in learning and in self-improvement, these curious wanderers were delighted to share knowledge and information.

The Hyksos were a tribe of several families, and each family patriarch was by tradition aged and wise. The core group of this tribe, the elders, were responsible for guarding ancient wisdom brought from the long-submerged continent of Mu. Perhaps their name "Musons" is where the ancient order of "masons" got its start. It is believed by some that the Ark of the Covenant is actually a relic from Lemuria, and this remarkable remnant tribe had custody of it.

It quickly became apparent to the aborigines in the valley that the Hyksos were content with less desirable lands and were not in the least warlike— though it was also apparent they would be a mighty foe if they were attacked. The newcomers offered improved-quality tools, utensils, and decorative artifacts for barter. Within a few years these Hyksos had gained the confidence and the respect of nearly every tribal group inhabiting the delta. Word spread that the elders of the

Hyksos had obtained wisdom beyond anything heretofore understood by the local populace.

The new group willingly shared much of their working knowledge on growing better crops, measuring the rise and fall of the all-important river, and establishing an accurate calendar for determining optimum planting and harvest times. It is only natural when people cooperate for the good of all that those with genuine ability gravitate to positions of leadership. The Hyksos, neither seeking it nor coveting it, became the leading tribe in the valley. Though they did not actively campaign for this leading role, the elders graciously assumed the responsibility that always accompanies leadership. Within a decade of their arrival, the Hyksos had calmly ushered in a period of great prosperity and well-being.

By their life-style, the Hyksos taught a philosophy of life. And tales of wondrous civilizations past were circulated, in which a purpose for striving for human perfection was outlined. The Hyksos believed that every human could eventually attain perfection by the practice of virtue and by making the effort to improve. This was not a new religion being introduced to the Nile valley. There were already a number of religions present that were steeped in tradition, and the Hyksos knew it to be unwise to try to change deeply held beliefs. However, the new thoughts on the nature of man were introduced, and parts of the philosophy were to show up thousands of years later in a series of papyri writings now popularly known as the *Egyptian Book of the Dead.*

At a peak period in the new prosperity about a decade after their arrival, the Hyksos suggested that life was so prosperous and harmonious that a grand monument to God and Man should be erected. They explained that the monument would also serve the entire delta as a practical clock and calendar while also serving as an inspiration to future generations. Typical of their style, the Hyksos also suggested that it would be a happy challenge to build a monument as perfectly as possible. It was surprisingly easy to get more volunteer labor than the overseers of the building project could house and feed in the vicinity of the plateau selected as the site by the elders. The technique of appealing to the noble nature of man gets excellent results. The area-wide project was agreed upon, and the workers listened in happy anticipation as the wise old patriarchs of the Hyksos, smiling and gentle, yet firm of purpose, outlined the tasks. Indeed they proposed a colossal structure.

Since these wise elders demonstrated amazing knowledge, no one doubted they could achieve what they planned. The workers toiled cheerfully and efficiently. No building techniques were used that were not physically available to the culture of the time. The elders did not sneak out in the dark of night and levitate the great blocks into place, nor did they secretly unveil a laser beam to cut the stones with the remarkable precision attained. Bronze tools were tipped with diorite, a stone second only to diamonds in hardness and found in abundance throughout Northern Africa. Large pieces of quartz crystal were ground into lenses that focused sunlight and generated a heat capable of melting stone. Ox blood provided the base for the remarkable cement, and water was used for leveling and also for transport. Locks and canals were built so the huge blocks could be floated to the building site, which is well away from the river's edge.

Perhaps the most important factor was that none of the workers harbored a doubt that such a monument could be built. Thoughts of failure, which tend to produce failure, were simply non-existent. It is absolutely amazing what people can do with a cheerful, positive, cooperative attitude and a group consciousness that reflects well-being. During planting and harvesting times the work on the Great Pyramid was set aside for the good of everyone.

Only the elders knew the design and purpose of the monument, so as it neared completion about eighty years after work began, none of the working people had a reasonable overview of the entire project. The people knew only that they had erected a "glorious light" for the benefit of all.

The elders in charge of the project, though extremely aged by our standards today, beamed their approval to one another when they sighted in the stars from the truncated top of the pyramid. Looking into the night sky, they determined that the meridian of the Great Pyramid passed precisely through the star designated as the toe of Castor in the constellation Gemini at exactly midnight on the autumnal equinox. The elders were pleased, their work was completed on schedule. This grandest of all monuments was topped off as we entered the astrological Age of Taurus. This coincides with the year 4699 B.C., as we will see later.

The great and glorious "light" stood silently,

yet brilliantly, above the Nile delta. It was surely a symbol of what man can do with harmony, co-operation, and joy. Within a few years the Hyksos had moved on as unobtrusively as they had arrived. A few remained to eventually form the nucleus of a secret society that guarded the grand monument. The Hyksos left behind a people far advanced from what they had been a century earlier.

As the centuries passed, the memory of the Hyksos became dimmer and dimmer, yet the glistening white limestone continued to harden and shine, polished by the weather. Though windswept sands piled up around its base, the Great Pyramid was the unmistakable guardian of the delta. About seven centuries after its completion, a powerful leader united the tribes of the upper and lower Nile valley, and ancient Egypt became the first truly organized political entity since the cataclysms. High above all the activity towered the majestic pyramid, forming a part of their heritage that these later Egyptians did not understand. The monument became sacred but little understood. The builders meant it that way—the time for understanding was far in the future.

The handful of Hyksos that remained in Egypt stayed in the background and carefully selected new members for their secret organization. These were the caretakers who checked the structure for damage during the early centuries and who stayed on to teach their "mysteries," or profound truths, to worthy students. It is believed by many that the Sphinx was built by members of this secret society, and there is a connecting link between the enigmatic Sphinx and the Great Pyramid. I do not believe this legend. The Great Pyramid's purpose does not require a connection with the Sphinx.

Archeologists have shown that the likeness of the face of the Sphinx and the likeness of Chephren, the alleged builder of the second pyramid, are nearly identical. The ramp to the second pyramid originates near the Sphinx, and there are a number of reasons to deduce that it was built far later than the Great Pyramid. Bob Vary, a friend of mine, who founded the Church of Nutrition and Mental Awareness in Chicago, suggested an interesting theory regarding the Sphinx and any possible connection with the Great Pyramid. He believes that because the Great Pyramid was sacred, no one, not even Pharaoh, dared to defile it publicly, so a deep underground passage was dug to it, and disguised by building the Sphinx over the opening.

This could be the passage system so many people feel exists between the Sphinx and the Great Pyramid. If this is fact, and the passage is uncovered, as predicted by Edgar Cayce and others, the finders are most likely to be highly disappointed. On the other hand, they might find the undiscovered remains of Pharaoh Khufu, who got credit for building the Great Pyramid.

Sometime after the third millennium before Christ, following another Hyksos "infiltration," a great king came to power in Egypt. Historians have enough evidence to believe his name was Zoser, and he is credited with being the first of the "pyramid builders." Zoser is said to have employed the fantastic genius Imhotep, who was probably a member of the secret society of Hermetics—the group originated by the Hyksos. Imhotep, it is believed, designed the "step pyramid" at Saqqara, the first edifice of this pyramidal shape to be built entirely of stone. The "step pyramid" resembles the famed Ziggurats of Babylon, which were also an offshoot of Hyksos teaching. Zoser started something that each successive Pharaoh tried to improve upon. It became the prestige thing to do for rulers to build huge pyramid-shaped tombs.

To justify the labor, which was not so cheerfully given as it had been more than a thousand years earlier, a rationale had to be developed by the priests. Pharaohs became gods incarnate, and the original chapters of the *Book of the Dead* were corrupted into funeral instructions for the higher classes. The easy-going, cheerful life-style of the ancient Hyksos had been supplanted by the need of the ruling classes to maintain power over others.

Finally, the Pharaoh we assume was named Khufu ascended the throne. By this time the rulers were obsessed with the idea of pyramid building as their means for immortality, and Khufu hit upon an idea that none of the others could ever surpass. He knew the Great Pyramid was the crowning achievement of man—also he was probably educated in part by members of the secret society—so he adopted this first wonder of the world as his own. Perhaps he did effect some repairs, as was recorded by his scribes on a stele belonging to one of his relatives, but he had absolutely nothing to do with it otherwise. Khufu took his name, "Glorious Light," from the pyramid and had his family temple and funeral plots erected around the base of the monument.

Because of the amount of time it would require to build the second pyramid, it is logical to assume that Khufu started the construction only to realize it would not be completed in his lifetime. The second pyramid was most likely well on its way during Khufu's 23-year reign, but rather than have his mummy lodged in an unfinished monument, which was actually nothing more than an attempt to copy the Great Pyramid, Khufu chose to have his remains stashed away elsewhere. Perhaps one day his funeral paraphernalia will be found if a tunnel from the Sphinx to the Great Pyramid is uncovered. By finding his remains, and the likewise missing remains of his son Khafra, or Chephren, we may indeed learn the "secret of the Great Pyramid" that so many would-be prophets are visualizing these days. We would learn that Khufu did not build it, he only borrowed it.

To support the borrowing theme, two things come to mind. First, Chephren's name is not inscribed anywhere within the second pyramid, which indicates that he was not solely responsible for its erection; second, it is noteworthy that the mastabas surrounding the Great Pyramid and believed to house the remains of Khufu's family members are far more precise in design and layout than are those around the bases of the other two Giza pyramids. Khufu took great pains to make his adoption of the grand monument acceptable and somewhat worthy. Ironically, only one small likeness of Khufu, who took such pains to secure his immortality, has ever been uncovered, but his descendants, Chephren and Mycernius, did very well for themselves, as shown by the excellent diorite statues of them that have been found.

The completion of the second pyramid literally marked the pinnacle of Egyptian pyramid building—and it is a far cry from the perfection of the original. It's obvious to me that the Great Pyramid's base was covered with sand when the copiers went to work because they overlooked the socket stones at each corner.

Mycernius, who followed Chephren, realized that he could not build so huge a monument, so he made a smaller, neater one—coating it with finely hewn slabs of granite.

Little by little as the art of pyramid building deteriorated, the powers of the priests grew until they actually held more sway over Egypt than the Pharaohs held. The secret society of Hermetics went further underground for safety's sake, and the Great Pyramid's real purpose was lost to all but a few elders. It is said that these Hermetics actually stored the golden Holy of Holies, around which Moses built the Ark of the Covenant, inside the main chamber of the Great Pyramid. According to scholars who looked into the matter, the Ark would fit perfectly within the granite sarcophagus that is still inside that chamber.

Nearly a thousand years after Khufu's time, a man named Joseph was sold into bondage by his brothers. Joseph worked his way up the social ladder and eventually brought his former tribe into Egypt. This was a major turning point for the nomadic Jews, whose religious zeal for one God instead of many can also be traced to Hykso influences around 4000 B.C. The Jews learned the advantages of a stable civilization. They learned to be masons and builders during nearly 400 years of bondage. During this period a Pharaoh named Ikhnaton ascended the throne of Egypt and tried to destroy the power of the Egyptian priests. Though he did a good job, the effects lasted only a short time, and in the end the priests came back with a vengeance. A few generations after Ikhnaton, when Egypt was a powerful, warring nation, a man named Moses, who knew all the secret doctrines of the ancient Hyksos, fulfilled his obligation to the overall plan, and guided the Jews out of Egypt and to their "promised land." The Jews were to finally settle in their own nation and establish the civilization that would usher in the world's greatest teacher. Meanwhile, the Great Pyramid glistened in the sunlight and patiently awaited its eventual recognition.

Though it is sketchy at best, there is a reference to the Great Pyramid in the Old Testament that appears to indicate a link between that structure and the plan that prepared the way for the most powerful single influence on earth—the advent of Christ. Jeremiah, a renowned prophet, pointed out that God "hast set signs and wonders in the land of Egypt, even unto this day."

Isaiah spoke of an "altar to the Lord in the midst of the land of Egypt," and also of a "pillar to the Lord at the border thereof." One need only look at the chart of the quadrant of the Nile delta to see that the Great Pyramid is situated at both the border and in the midst of the land.

So while there is apparent mention of the Great Pyramid in Biblical texts, there is little mention of it elsewhere in ancient literature. Herodotus wrote a great deal about the rulers who tyrannically forced their people to build the huge stone monuments to their vanity, and in so doing he perhaps tainted the magnificence of the Great Pyramid. Yet the ancient Greeks wisely chose it as the "first wonder of the world."

Time continued its relentless march, and the sands of the Libyan desert piled higher around the base of the ancient pyramids. Great men and great cities rose up, beat their chests in the sun, and faded into musty reference books while the Great Pyramid glistened on. Alexander the Great, Caesar and Cleopatra, mighty Carthage and splendid Byzantium all blossomed and died before the perfection of the Pyramid was blemished by the outworkings of man's free will and ignorance.

The Moslems came to rule the Middle East, and the Caliph of Baghdad was now Pharaoh. Al Mamun, whose father Harun El Rashid inspired the tales of the Arabian Nights, was told by his viziers that the secrets of the universe were contained within the Great Pyramid and that riches galore would be found if he were to penetrate its shining exterior. Al Mamun had his men tunnel into the massive limestone edifice, and eventually they struck upon the passage system. All their effort was matched by their ignorance—once they found all the passages, they wailed in disappointment. No gold, no jewels, no secret scrolls— nothing but exquisite architecture unmatched anywhere in the world. But who cares about architecture when one is searching for riches?

The Moslems ripped out the entrance doorway and opened the sacred monument to bats and rodents, humidity and vandals. Earthquakes rocked Egypt some years later, and needing stone for reconstruction, the Arabs found the monuments at Giza to be excellent quarries. The beautiful and polished Tura limestone was ripped away and used to build bridges, roads, and the great Mosque of Cairo.

Stripped of its beauty, ravaged by time, earthquake, and man, the Great Pyramid patiently waited to serve its purpose. The time was approaching.

What manner of intuition would cause an Oxford scholar of seventeenth-century England to wander across the continent and part of North Africa in search of a unit of measure? That was the quest of John Greaves, professor of astronomy at Oxford in 1637, who stood in awe before the Great Pyramid, and then proceeded to do battle with the bat guano and stench to measure portions of the interior. With the work of Greaves, who wrote a book on "pyramidographia," the beginnings of the fantastic decoding process were set in motion. Was it accidental?

Between 1647 and 1761, while a new nation was rapidly evolving on the North American continent, prominent investigators from the European centers of learning trudged across the Giza plateau and the ruins of the ancient civilization. What could possibly have been the draw? What merited all this scholarly attention to the now jagged and worn blocks of limestone once proudly covered with a glistening shield? Perhaps the single most powerful attraction is that inner gnawing some men have for information lodged deep in the group consciousness of mankind—a nagging urge to seek meaning where confusion holds sway. That the Great Pyramid was part of mystic lore cannot be denied. The Founding Fathers of the United States saw fit to include it on the Great Seal of the United States. We can all view the end result of this curious heraldry on each of our dollar bills today.

That the Masonic Order was primarily responsible for the lore cannot be doubted. The U.S. Seal was originated in a series of committee meetings after 1780. The same emblematic idea was used in 1776 by the Bavarian Order of Illuminati, an offshoot of the Freemasons.

Whatever the reasons, scholars began probing around the Great Pyramid with more than idle curiosity after the path was broken by Greaves. A British consul at Algiers, Nathaniel Davison, did some additional interior exploration in 1763, and finally Napoleon Bonaparte conquered Egypt and ushered in his small army of "savants," or scholars. The French were the first to survey the site of the Great Pyramid trigonometrically. And it was the French who discovered two of the "socket" stones at the base corners that further distinguish the Great Pyramid from all others. The builders embedded stones into the plateau at each corner to ensure alignment and structural strength.

After Waterloo, the British returned to dominate the study of Egyptology, and they brought with them something the French did not have— something that gave them a definite edge in deciphering the message geometrically outlined by the Great Pyramid. The British used the inch, the French the meter. As it turns out, the inch is more exacting and more ancient than the meter, and is, in fact, the key to the Great Pyramid's purpose.

CHAPTER FOUR

Revelations in Measures

Men of science have been compelled to look into the mystique of the Great Pyramid because everything about the monument seems to call out for scientific scrutiny. The size, shape, precision, and orientation have shouted loudly to all with the ability to understand: "Hey, look at me! Pay attention to me, I'm amazing!" No other edifice on earth has attracted so much careful attention, yet not a single word is carved on its walls. No doubt the wise Hykso elders intended it so. But why?

The word "pyramid" itself gives us a clue. It is derived from the Greek "pyramidos" or, roughly, "fire in the middle." The Greeks may have derived their word from ancient Hebrew-Chaldeac "urrim midden," which translates as "lights-measures." The ancient Egyptian word for pyramid was "khuti" or "khufu" and is said to mean "glorious light." The Coptic word for the structure was "pirimit," which meant "the tenth measure in numbers." Across the Atlantic Ocean the Mayans called their pyramids "pirhua manco," which is not only phonetically similar, but it translates as "revealer of light." The inference made here is that these clues indicate that the Great Pyramid has revelations in its measures. And it is precisely in the measurements that a scientific message has been decoded.

However, in order to decode or appreciate the science of the Great Pyramid, the investigators had to have knowledge at least equal to that of the builders. Our culture had to understand gravitational astronomy to a refined degree in order to recognize that it was also thoroughly understood by the Great Pyramid's designer. If we did not fully understand the universal geometric relationship between diameter and circumference, the number called "pi," how could we have realized that the Great Pyramid's exterior measurements monumentalize it? The Great Pyramid's proportions and measurements deliver an eloquent scientific message without the problems of semantics or interpretation. It has been agreed by scientific minds that the very best way to communicate the fact of intelligence where language would have no meaning whatsoever is to convey knowledge of universal geometric relationships—such as pi.

It is in the measures of the Great Pyramid that astounding science is manifested. Napoleon's "savant," E. François Jomard, deduced that the Great Pyramid builders knew enough astronomy, geodesy, and geometry to have accurately measured the circumference of the earth and monumentalized it in the structure. What the French scientists missed was picked up by the British, because the British had one tiny advantage over the other European scientists: they used the inch as their unit of measure. And so did the builders of the Great Pyramid. In fact the British apparently inherited all their units of measure from peoples whose ancestry is somehow directly linked to the mysterious Hyksos. Of course, if you consult your encyclopedia, you will not find this statement corroborated. If you try to find out the origin of the inch from reference books and contact with experts, here's what you'll discover: "Britannica, page 370, volume 23 . . . Since the available material is incomplete and inconsistent, conflicting interpretations have been very common. . . . It *seems likely* that units of measurement first used in prehistory were those of length and that they derived from parts of the human body—foot, hand, etc. . . . The inch was one/twelfth the Roman foot introduced to Britain."

That last sentence sounds rather final, but it really isn't. The inch may have been taken from the old British foot, which may have been the length of some king's foot, without a shoe. Or, it may have been the length of three barleycorns, or some king's nose . . .

I'm digressing for a moment to air a complaint about the methods used by our erudite academicians whose opinions rule science and the statements in our reference books. The tendency of the reader of that reference information is to skim over the phrases like "seems likely," which are italicized here but not in the encyclopedia, and to accept as final the conclusive-sounding statement in the final line. The authoritative experts in any field of study do not enjoy having their expertise tarnished—and this is normal enough. So they go to great length to sound authoritative, when, in fact, they have no real authority. The best, or worst, example I've run across is from the Encyclopedia Americana under "phallic ritual." This is considered a widespread aspect of primitive culture, so this book of "knowledge" has this to say about it:

"It is *impossible* to trace its origin, which *probably* had a spontaneous origin among different races, although its source is *undoubtedly* Eastern [italics mine]."

There, in one sentence, you have pompous expertise epitomized. The experts have no way to be sure of the truth, so they cover themselves with the "impossible" clause, then hedge with the "probably," and finally make their opinion into fact with "undoubtedly" Eastern.

The technique works. In fact, I'm using it myself whenever I'm certain of my opinion. So much for the digression, the inch is at hand, and it's of the utmost importance.

To be truly scientific, it is believed that linear measures must be commensurate with the size of our planet. For this reason astronomers took great pains to calculate the distance from the equator to the North Pole along the meridian at Dunkirk, France; then they divided that distance into 10 million equal parts and came up with the "meter." This unit of measure (39.37 inches) became the linear standard for the world, excepting the vast English-speaking part of it. The English-speaking world doggedly clings to its "unscientific" inch system, and only in recent years have we started to succumb to the temptations of the decimal system employed in the metric system, but not so much to the metric system itself.

It has been determined, finally, that no two meridians on our lumpy, oblate planet would measure precisely the same, so another "scientific" source for the meter was needed. Today the meter's length is determined to be 1,650,763.73 wavelengths of the orange-red radiation of krypton, under specified conditions.

It can be clearly shown that the "year-circle" described in inches was utilized by both the builders of the Great Pyramid and the builders of the monument at Stonehenge, England. The inner circle of the ancient British monument is a year-circle because it has a circumference that measures the number of days in a solar year. Without laboring the point at this time, it can be shown that the British Isles inherited a basic unit of linear measure from the ancestors of the mysterious Druids who could well have been Hyksos, for all we know. Admittedly, this is only a theory, but it makes good sense—especially as we pursue the inch and its use in the Great Pyramid.

Sir John Herschel, an eminent British astronomer of the nineteenth century, determined that the "pyramid inch" is a hairline longer than the inch we use today. Herschel noted that this unit of measure (1.0011 inches) was commensurate with the polar diameter of the earth. The polar-diameter inch, or "pyramid inch" is precisely one-five hundred millionth the distance from the North Pole to the South Pole through the center of the earth. This unit of measure is embodied in so many places throughout the Great Pyramid's geometric system that it is beyond a doubt the basic unit of measure utilized by the builders. Immediately one wonders how they managed to calculate the earth's polar diameter so accurately. The Great Pyramid designer thus calculated the earth's diameter to be 7899.31 miles. Herschel and Colonel Clark of the British Ordinance Department calculated it to be 7899.23 miles, and astronomer R. S. Ball later calculated it to be 7899.42 miles. Curiously, the ancient calculation is equidistant between these two later calculations. Today our orbiting satellites tell us the distance is 7899.8 miles. Perhaps some ice has been added to the South Pole since the pyramid builders calculated the distance. I certainly don't want to bet that they were in error.

No wonder the great French astronomer, the Abbé Moreaux, said: "The British are correct in keeping their inch rather than joining the metric system." Moreaux, after a lengthy study of the Great Pyramid wrote: "We have called to our aid all the sciences; we have spent centuries in labors and concurrent efforts; perfected our technique; continued with slow perseverance the tasks of our predecessors; pushed to an unimaginable point the exactness of our calculations, and ended finally in discovering something that was known 4,500 years ago!"

Not only did the ancient pyramid builders know that the most precise line of reference for basing a standard linear measure is the earth's polar diameter or axis of rotation, but they were able to calculate the distance with stunning accuracy. To obtain a larger unit of measure, these ancients then divided the distance from the pole to the equator into 10 million equal parts and came up with a cubit of 25 polar-diameter inches. The Hyksos' influence on ancient cultures is ever present. In the case of the cubit of 25 polar-diameter (pd) inches we find it was considered sacred by the prophets and leaders of Israel.

Egyptologists today reject the pd-inch thesis, despite the remarkable geometric proofs. Let's take the Great Pyramid's geometric makeup, step by step.

Basil Stewart, author of *History of the Great Pyramid*, put it this way: "The Great Pyramid was built to monumentalize the geometry of the circle, thereby introducing the incommensurable factor denoting the relationship between diameter and circumference, expressed usually as 3.14159, but can be carried to hundreds of decimals without reaching finality. This basis of the year-circle was utilized to represent the number of days in the year, another incommensurable number, and all the other orbital values of the earth—its distance from the sun, the value of precession, and other astronomical data."

In the case of the Great Pyramid, the year-circle has a circumference of 36,524.22 pd-inches. That number just happens to be the number of days in a solar year, times 100, or the number of days in a century. Taking that circumference and designing a square base with a perimeter equal to that number of pd-inches we come up with a base square of the Great Pyramid. If we made the vertical height of a pyramid with that same base perimeter equal to the radius of the same year-circle, we obtain the height of the Great Pyramid. Essentially, the entire structural design, including the interior passages and chambers are set out from this apparently simple but fantastic geometric application. See Diagram One. (Page four of insert section.)

Using the year-circle as a basis, we find the base sides of the pyramid will be one-fourth 36,524.22 pd-inches, or 9,131.05 pd-inches. This figure converts to 755 feet, 9½ inches, or roughly 755.7 feet. According to the acknowledged authority on the pyramids of Egypt today, Dr. I. E. S. Edwards, the base side measurements of the Great Pyramid are as follows: north side—755.43 feet; south—756.08 feet; east—755.88 feet; and west—755.77 feet. It's plain that despite the ravages of time, the Great Pyramid's measurements are within a few inches of perfect. It is also notable that most experts surmise the west base side was the first one laid out by the builders, and it is this base side measure that is within thousandths of an inch of matching the year-circle geometry.

In Diagram One (Page four of insert section), Basil Stewart describes all the geometry of the circle-pyramid. You can see that line AF represents the height of the pyramid. That height is the equivalent of the radius of the year-circle, or 5,813 pd-inches. Expressed geometrically, this means the value of the vertical height must be in proportion to twice the base side as the diameter is to the circumference—or, AF = 18,262 : 1 : 3.14159. The resultant 5,813 pd-inches is equal to 481.4 feet, which is precisely what Dr. Edwards tells us the Great Pyramid, with an apex, would measure.

This formula will make the slope of the angles 51 degrees, 51 minutes, 14.3 seconds of arc, and that's the angle of the exterior casing stones found in their original positions near the base of the Great Pyramid.

One of the "sins" of pyramidologists who become overenthusiastic about the science embodied in the Great Pyramid's measures is to claim that this circle-pyramid geometry "squares the circle." Actually, the geometry does offer a practical means for *nearly* squaring the circle, but because the value of pi cannot be exactly determined, a circle cannot be truly squared. According to Stewart, there is no geometrical method of drawing a straight line equal to the circumference of a given circle, but the Great Pyramid's geometry comes close enough by defining equality of boundaries. The dotted line on Diagram One (see insert section) illustrates a mathematical fact. Though the year-circle has the same perimeter as the square pyramid base, a circle always contains the greater area. The area of the square base is enclosed by the dotted line, and it will have a diameter of 10,303.3 pd-inches as opposed to the year-circle's diameter of 11,626 pd-inches.

It's evident that the sciences of geometry and gravitational astronomy were well known to the designer of the Great Pyramid. This geometry clearly shows a knowledge of mathematics not even fully comprehended by Pythagoras. Our reference books tell us that Archimedes first calculated the area of a circle, some time in the third century B.C. Obviously, our record books are in error. Our view of history prior to 3000 B.C. is distorted. One is forced by reason to conclude that the knowledge of geometry, mathematics, and astronomy demonstrated by the design of the Great Pyramid was not possessed by those people we call ancient Egyptians. Adding substance to the theory that the Great Pyramid was built by a remnant culture (Hyksos) from previous civilizations is this observation by Dr. Joseph A. Seiss, prominent American pyramidologist:

"Never was it in the power of the ancient Egyptians to understand, much less to originate and enunciate, the science found in the Great Pyramid. Other pyramids were *of* Egypt, but they are totally lacking in all these elements of intellectuality. We look in vain for any traces that they ever understood the mathematical "pi" much less construct so original a symbol for it. There is no doubt they never had any appreciation of the pyramid's system of numbers, or knew anything of the sun's distance, or the earth's form."

There is much more math and geometry embodied in the Great Pyramid's dimensions, and there is a great deal more science embodied than math, geometry, and gravitational astronomy. The Appendixes at the end of this book describe other sciences, today's faddish discoveries, and even games people have played with the scientific mystique of the Great Pyramid.

For our present objective, that of getting directly to the highest purpose of the Great Pyramid, we can be content with the year-circle geometry as the essential design. Having seen the exterior dimensions worked out, we now explore the interior system of passages and chambers, a system found nowhere else on earth except within the confines of the Great Pyramid.

CHAPTER FIVE

The Interior System

Before the Arabs under Al Mamun tunneled into the north face of the Great Pyramid and opened its interior passages and chambers to the elements, the interior system was unmarred geometric and literary perfection in stone. The system is so unusual that Egyptologists cannot accept the idea that the construction was designed completely and purposely. They feel the arrangement of the passages and chambers "must be considered in conjunction with its structural development." The scholarly view is that the interior system of the Great Pyramid underwent "transformations" as the builders changed their minds during the actual construction. This viewpoint is, in my opinion, as illogical as the tombic theory itself. The geometry of the year-circle used for the exterior is continued trigonometrically to outline the interior system—it is so mathematically precise that it had to have been predetermined by the designer.

Referring to Diagram One (insert page four), let's design the interior, step by step, using the year-circle of 36,524.22 pd-inches:

To obtain the slope of the passages, describe the square and circle, PQRS having equal area to triangle ABC, or the area of section. Project the side of square PS to T, which meets our year-circle circumference. Now join TF and the angle. TFC gives the precise angle of the slope of the descending passage, 26 degrees, 18 minutes, 10 seconds. To obtain the slope for the ascending passage, trisect the line EF at H and K (notice you have established the floor lines for the two upper chambers with the trisection). Bisect line FG at D. Through point D, draw line DM parallel to FT, cutting the circle at I. Point I is the juncture of the passages, as they are in actuality, and DM locates the ascending passage on the calculated slope of angle. Line IH describes the ascending passage system from juncture to the floor of the main chamber. The entire interior system is thus geometrically and trigonometrically outlined.

The system does not rest directly in the center of the north-south axis. It is deliberately offset to the left, and this matter is thoroughly discussed in Chapter Six. The diagram is the east-west section, and you may notice that the large gallery of the ascending passage, a magnificent bit of architecture commonly called the Grand Gallery, ends right on the axis line, or dead center. The main chamber is, like the entrance, offset to the left of center a definite and deliberate number of pd-inches.

The entrance is now a gaping hole about fifty-five feet from the base of the northern face of the Great Pyramid. To avoid contradiction, here is the precise description of the interior system given by Dr. I. E. S. Edwards in *The Pyramids of Egypt:*

The entrance is in the north face at a height of about 55 feet, measured vertically, above ground level. It is not situated exactly midway across the face, but at a point about 24 feet east of center. From the entrance a corridor, measuring about 3 feet, 5 inches in width and 3 feet 11 inches in height, descends at a gradient of 26° 31′ 24″ first through the core of the pyramid and then through the rock. At a distance of about 345 feet from the original entrance the corridor becomes level and continues horizontally for a further 29 feet before terminating in a chamber. . . . On the west side of the level section of the corridor, near the entrance to the chamber, there is a recess, the cutting of which was never completed. The chamber also is unfinished, its trenched floors and rough walls resembling a quarry. A square pit sunk in the floor may represent the first stage of an unfulfilled project for deepening the chamber. According to Byse and Perring, who measured the chamber in 1838, its dimensions are: height 11 feet, 6 inches; east-west, 46 feet; north-south, 27 feet, 1 inch.

In the south wall of the chamber, opposite the entrance, there is an opening to a blind passage, roughly hewn in the rock and obviously unfinished. The presence of this passage suggests that, if the original plan had been executed, there would have been a second chamber beyond the first and connected with it by a corridor. Such an arrangement would have as a parallel the Northern Stone Pyramid at Dahshur, the main difference being that in the latter the second chamber lies directly beneath the apex and the first to the north of it, whereas in the Great Pyramid both chambers would have been situated south of a point perpendicularly under the apex.

I am going to continue with Dr. Edwards' detailed description, and also his digressions so you may see the reasoning of scholars who are convinced that the Great Pyramid was a tomb—they are surely sincere.

It is of some interest to compare the half-finished rock-chamber with the brief but graphic description of the subterranean part of the Great Pyramid given to Herodotus when he visited Egypt in the middle of the fifth century B.C. Beneath the pyramid, he was told, were vaults constructed on a kind of island, which was surrounded by water brought from the Nile by a canal. On this island the body of Cheops was said to lie. No trace, however, of either the canal or the island has yet been found, and it is most unlikely that they ever existed. Although the pyramid had *almost certainly* [italics added] been opened and its contents plundered long before the time of Herodotus, it may easily have been closed again during the Saite Period, when a number of ancient monuments were restored. The story which Herodotus relates—the veracity of which he does not claim to have confirmed from his own observations—may well have been embroidered by generations of pyramid guides extending over the greater part of two centuries.

At the time when the decision was made to alter the original project and to substitute a burial-chamber in the body of the pyramid for the one under construction in the rock, the superstructure had already been built to a height of several feet. A hole was therefore cut in the masonry roof of the earlier descending corridor at a point about 60 feet from the entrance and a new ascending corridor was hewn upwards through the core. The mouth of this corridor was filled, after the burial, with a slab of limestone, so that it became indistinguishable from the remainder of the roof at the upper end of the descending corridor. The block could not, however, have been securely fastened, because it collapsed when Ma'mun's men were boring their tunnel near by. According to Moslem historians it was the noise made by the fall of this block to the floor of the descending corridor which enabled the tunnellers to locate the pyramid corridors, their previous operations having been directed too far to the west.

The ascending corridor, which is approximately 129 feet in length, corresponds in width and height with the descending corridor; its gradient of 26° 2′ 30″ also tallies to within a fraction of a degree. At its lower end, immediately above the gap left by the missing limestone slab, are three large plug-blocks made of granite and placed one behind the other. These plugs, which completely fill the original corridor, were by-passed by Ma'mun's men, who simply cut a passage through the softer limestone of the west wall as far as a point beyond the uppermost plug. Borchardt, while making a detailed study of the walls of this corridor, observed that the stones at the lower end were laid approximately parallel with the ground, whereas nearly all those at the upper end were parallel with the gradient of the corridor. From this fact he deduced that the point at which the angle changed marked the height to which the pyramid had already been built when it was decided to transfer the tomb-chamber to the superstructure. Borchardt also noticed that the joints of the stones at the lower end were irregular, whereas the stones at the upper end fitted closely—a feature which certainly supports his contention that the lower part of the corridor was cut through rough core masonry already laid, while the upper part was built *para passu* with the construction of the pyramid. The only stones in the upper part which are not laid parallel with the gradient are the so-called "girdle stones," a name used to describe either single stones or two stones, one above the other, through which the corridor has been hewn. These "girdle stones," placed at regular intervals of 17 feet, 2 inches, may offer a clue to the structural composition of the Great Pyramid. . . .

When the ascending corridor was being constructed, the builders probably intended the burial-chamber to occupy a position in the center of the superstructure and at no great height above ground level. Such a chamber was actually built at the end of a passage leading from the top of the ascending corridor. Called by the Arabs the "Queen's Chamber"—a misnomer which it has retained—this chamber lies exactly midway between the north and south sides of the pyramid. Its measurements are 18 feet, 10 inches from east to west and 17 feet, 2 inches from north to south. It has a pointed roof, which rises to a height of 20 feet, 5 inches. In the east wall there is a niche with corbelled sides; its original depth was only 3 feet, 5 inches, but the back has now been cut away by treasure seekers. Its height is 15 feet, 4 inches, and the width at the base is 5 feet, 2 inches. Presumably it was designed to contain a statue of the king, which may, however, never have been placed in position.

There are many indications that work on the Queen's Chamber was abandoned before it had been completed. The floor, for instance, is exceedingly rough; if the chamber had been finished it would probably have been paved with finer stone. Again, in the north and south walls there are small rectangular apertures from which shafts run horizontally for a distance of about 6 feet, 6 inches and then turn upwards at an angle of approximately 30°. These apertures were not cut at the time when the chamber was built—an omission which can only be explained on the hypothesis that the chamber was never finished—but in 1872 by an engineer named Waynman Dixon, who had been led to suspect the existence of the shafts by their presence in the King's Chamber above. Unlike those in the King's Chamber, however, the shafts leading from the

Queen's Chamber seem to have had no outlet in the outer surface of the pyramid; the absence of such an outlet provides further evidence of an alteration in the original plan. Possibly the same explanation also accounts for the different levels in the floor of the passage which connected the ascending corridor with the chamber. At first the passage is only 3 feet, 9 inches in height, but nearer the chamber a sudden drop in the floor increases its height to 5 feet, 8 inches.

The abandonment of the Queen's Chamber led to the construction of two of the most celebrated architectural works which have survived from the Old Kingdom, namely the Grand Gallery and the King's Chamber. The Grand Gallery was built as a continuation of the ascending corridor. It is 153 feet in length and 28 feet in height. Its walls of polished limestone rise vertically to a height of 7 feet, 6 inches; above that level each of the seven courses projects inwards about three inches beyond the course on which it rests, thus forming a corbel vault of unparelleled dimensions. The space between the uppermost course on each side, measuring 3 feet, 5 inches in width, is spanned by roofing slabs, every one of which is laid at a slightly steeper angle than the gradient of the gallery. Sir Flinders Petrie, commenting on this method of laying the slabs, says it was done "in order that the lower edge of each stone should hitch like a pawl into a ratchet cut in the top of the wall; hence no stone can press on the one below it, so as to cause a cumulative pressure all down the roof; and each stone is separately upheld by the side walls across which it lies." At the foot of each wall a flat-topped ramp, 2 feet in height and 1 foot, 8 inches in width, extends along the whole length of the gallery. A passage measuring, like the roof, 3 feet, 5 inches in width runs between the two ramps. At the lower end of this passage there is now a gap, caused by the removal of stones which formerly linked the floor of the passage with that of the ascending corridor and also covered the mouth of the horizontal passage leading to the Queen's Chamber. In the gap, the lowest stone of the western ramp has been removed, revealing a shaft which descends partly perpendicularly and partly obliquely, first through the core of the pyramid and then through the rock, until it emerges in the west wall of the descending corridor. . . .

A high step at the upper end of the Grand Gallery gives access to a low and narrow passage leading to the King's Chamber. About a third of the distance along its length the passage is heightened and enlarged into a kind of antechamber, the south, east and west walls of which are composed of red granite. . . .

The King's Chamber, built entirely of granite, measures 34 feet, 4 inches from east to west, 17 feet, 2 inches from north to south, and 19 feet, 1 inch in height. In the north and south walls, at a height of about 3 feet above the floor, are the rectangular apertures of shafts which differ from those of the Queen's Chamber only in penetrating the core of the pyramid to the outer surface, the northern shaft at an angle of 31° and the southern one at an angle of 45°. The object of these shafts is not known with certainty; they may have been designed for ventilation of the chamber or for some religious purpose which is still open for conjecture. Near the west wall stands a lidless rectangular sarcophagus which once contained the King's body, probably enclosed within an inner coffin of wood. In appearance it is rough, many of the scratches made by the saw when cutting it being still clearly visible. Sir Flinders Petrie discovered that the width of the sarcophagus was about an inch greater than the width of the ascending corridor at its mouth; he therefore concluded that it must have been placed in position while the chamber was being built.

The roof of the King's Chamber has no exact architectural parallel. Above its flat ceiling, which is composed of nine slabs weighing in aggregate about 400 tons, there are five separate compartments, the ceilings of the first four being flat and the fifth having a pointed roof. The purpose of this construction, it appears, was to eliminate any risk of the ceiling of the chamber collapsing under the weight of the superincumbent masonry. Whether such extreme precautions were required by the character of the building may be debatable; they have, however, been justified by subsequent events. Every one of the massive slabs of granite in the ceiling of the chamber and many of those in the relieving compartments have been cracked—presumably by an earthquake—but none has yet collapsed.

The preceding was a thorough description of the interior system of the Great Pyramid, and I included it almost in its entirety so that we could discuss some of the reasoning.

Scholars, like Ludwig Borchardt, who along with Sir Flinders Petrie, was referred to by Dr. Edwards, have argued about those three huge granite plugs where the ascending passage commences. Engineers and architects will tell you that those plugs could not have been slid down the corridor and used to close off the corridor after the Pharaoh's mummy was laid to rest. To slide those cubes of granite down the somewhat rough corridor would require at least 3/4-inch clearance all the way around the perimeter of each plug and a set of very good quality rollers. There is about 1/4-inch clearance around the plugs, and structural engineers who have looked at it agree they were built in place. This means the builders plugged their passages to their major chambers before they built them.

Whether the Hykso builders altered their construction is really a moot point. Perhaps during the course of the work some eager workers covered the portion of the pyramid where the chamber was to go—or better, perhaps it was easier in the long run to lay all the blocks in that particular course of masonry, and to then cut the corridor out where it was wanted. My argument is that a change in construction does not mean the designer changed original intent. The geometric outline seems to hold to logic far better than the deductions of Borchardt, evidence of construction alterations notwithstanding.

The small air shafts really pose a problem for orthodox Egyptologists; mummies certainly don't need air. It is also strange that the builders would "abandon" work on one chamber and then construct, unplanned yet, two of the grandest architectural works of antiquity. And, finally, I find it more than curious that the builders of the Great Pyramid, if they were working for Khufu a mere generation ahead of Chephren's workers who built the second pyramid, took such fantastic precautions with the ceiling slabs of the King's Chamber while the second pyramid's main chamber, under a lot more rock, has no such precautions.

Enough said. The geometry is too perfect to have been accidental, and there is a lot more evidence indicating that the interior system of the Great Pyramid has a purpose far nobler than housing the mummy of some vain ruler who didn't have the wherewithal to build the structure in the first place.

The system of passages and chambers within the Great Pyramid has a replica in literature. This literature is probably the oldest we have any record of, and it is commonly, and erroneously, called the *Egyptian Book of the Dead*. The *Book of the*

Dead has been translated by two scholars, the first was W. Marsham Adams of Oxford in 1897; the second, Dr. E. A. Wallis Budge. I find the first translation more logical and understandable; the second appears to me to be more of a rationale for the accepted views of history. The material for these translations comes from 189 chapters of funeral rite papyri found at various spots throughout the Nile valley. Some of these chapters are so old that they were recorded on the sarcophagus of Queen Khnemnefert, of the eleventh dynasty (2400 B.C.) Hieroglyphs state that a chapter of the *Book of the Dead* was *discovered* during the reign of Hesep-ti, about 4000 B.C.

To make a long and complicated translation short, let's consider this oversimplified, but in my opinion accurate, version of what the *Book of the Master of the House of Hidden Places* has to say. This is the translated title according to Adams in 1897.

The *Book of the Master* and the Great Pyramid describe the same path for every individual who lives and dies, then reincarnates again and again to learn the lessons of life. The one tells the story in words, the other in stone.

Every Ego, or Ka as the Egyptians called the discrete bundle of mental energy that makes up a person, descends into incarnation from another plane, and as the incarnation begins—as the child takes its first breath—the Ego loses all conscious memory of its previous lifetime. As one enters the Great Pyramid, it is on a descending angle. There is one hieroglyph inscribed in the limestone above the entrance—it is best translated as "horizon of heaven." This corresponds to the allegory in stone.

79

As each of us descends into life, the horizon of heaven narrows and we emerge in darkness.

We invariably reach a point in our descent into life and its unknowns where we may choose to elevate ourselves and begin the ascending path that ultimately returns to the Creator. However, the "Gate of Ascent" is blocked; the elevation of one's character is difficult. The way is blocked, and it is much easier to cease the attempt and drift along a descending slant, remaining in the dark regarding life's purposes. About sixty feet from the entrance, we find the ascending passage leading upward into the heart of the Great Pyramid, and the Gate of Ascent is plugged with those three cubes of granite, built deliberately into place.

Those souls or Egos that do not make the struggle to grow upward through the gate of ascent will continue to descend in darkness. They cannot know, for they descend further and further from the light until finally they reach the "chamber of upside downness," the chamber of "chaos." There are false indications that lead one to believe there is another way out, but these routes lead nowhere. The Ego in this chamber of chaos has no choice but to die in darkness, or climb all the way back up to the Gate of Ascent and make the struggle. All is not lost when one dies in "unknowingness" because he will be incarnated again, and again, and again so that he may choose to elevate—but the choice must be his own.

In the Great Pyramid, after you reach the granite plugs or the Gate of Ascent, you can continue descending for more than 360 feet in total darkness and close quarters until you finally reach the subterranean chamber carved out of the rocky plateau directly below the Pyramid's apex. Now, that took quite a bit of planning! The builders had to excavate the descending passage and chamber before they could pile up the stones to make the Pyramid. The theory that the plans were changed as the Pyramid was built becomes still harder to accept. In any case, this dark chamber is unique. The ceiling is dressed and relatively smooth, the floor is rough and unfinished—it's upside down, the chamber of chaos or upside-downness. There is what appears to be another corridor, but it leads to a dead end; there is what appears to be a well shaft or corridor leading straight down, but it too is a dead end. Is this chaos? A chamber built upside down with passages to nowhere!

Turning back to the Gate of Ascent, the Ego now incarnate makes the choice to strive for human perfection. He does not know at this point that perfection, rejoining the Creator, is what he is seeking, but he follows an inner urging that demands that he elevate himself. This inner urging is a "divine discontentment," very much like nature's urging to a caterpillar, which causes metamorphosis and beautiful butterflies. The aspiring individual makes his way through the Gate of Ascent and finds himself in the "Hall of Truth in Darkness." Once you make the effort, you can feel the ascent, but though you are on the right path, it is not immediately made easy—you must continue to make great effort.

In the Great Pyramid, once beyond the granite plugs you still must practically crawl along because the passage or corridor is still narrow and confining. It's also dark, but it does not become progressively darker as does the descending passage. You are moving upward through the Hall of Truth in Darkness.

Your physical life may expire at any point along the way, but you retain in your Egoic memory the lessons that brought you to the particular plateau of advancement along the path you have made—making it easier for you to choose the proper circumstances of life to incarnate into the next time around. The various plateaus of advancement are indicated by the "girdle stones" found every 17 feet 2 inches. It's quite noticeable that the distance of 17 feet 2 inches is also the dimension of the north-south floors in the two major chambers.

As you work your way upward along the Hall of Truth in Darkness, you will reach a corridor leading you toward a major plateau of Egoic development. You enter the "Chamber of New Birth," or "Second Birth." In this chamber you may take stock of all you have learned during your ascent in darkness, and there will be a realization of what you are struggling toward—a new awareness or consciousness of the purpose of all the effort. You will be filled with joy and new resolve to continue the ascent toward the Creator.

Armed with your new consciousness—cosmic consciousness some like to call it—you return to the ascending passage and suddenly emerge into the "Hall of Truth in Light." The grand gallery stands before you, magnificent, spacious, filled with the promise of glory.

Every phrase or name for the chambers or passages is translated directly from the *Book of the Master*, and it is obvious that each fits the interior system of the Great Pyramid perfectly.

Let's look at the cleverness of the symbolism in the actual construction. You are climbing upward in the narrow ascending passage, or Hall of Truth in Darkness. You are crouching and practically crawling along so you cannot see what is above; therefore when you reach the juncture of the corridor leading to the Queen's Chamber, or the Chamber of New Birth, it grasps your attention before you notice the Grand Gallery looming just above. Returning from your visit to the Queen's Chamber, your motion is going to take you naturally upward into the Grand Gallery as you emerge from the slanted corridor entrance. You now can stand up and stretch your limbs and move upward more easily in the huge, two-story gallery. It is indeed the Hall of Truth in Light.

As the joyous, growing Ego reaches the upper end of the Hall of Truth in Light, he must climb a great step before he can stand on a level floor. All your effort has brought you, finally, to the floor of the temple. You are on the verge of what the Buddhists and Hindus have called "liberation." You have almost reached the pinnacle of this round of existence; once you pass through the "Chamber of the Triple Veil" before you, you need never incarnate to the physical level again— your Egoic growth will be accomplished on higher levels of existence from this point on.

The Chamber of the Triple Veil obviously has three parts to it. According to the *Book of the Master*, the first part is "inner conflict," the second part is "truce in chaos," and the third part is "final tribulation and humility."

Let's look at the actual construction in the Great

Pyramid. At the upper end of the Grand Gallery is a great step of limestone and once you climb up onto it, you are standing on the floor level of the main chamber, or King's Chamber. However, to enter, you must stoop down again and enter another cramped corridor. After the magnificent ascent in the Grand Gallery, it's no wonder one wants to balk a little before stooping to enter the narrow, confining corridor. It's certainly symbolic of inner conflict. You only crawl for a few feet in this first "veil," and you can stand up inside a small antechamber. You get a break in the confinement, and you can reflect on your reaction to the confining entrance. You are also standing directly above the Chamber of Chaos hundreds of feet below, and perhaps as you are getting this second "veil" of "truce," you can reflect on the millions of Egos, exactly like you, who have yet to make the ascent. Ahead lies the third veil, and once again you are forced to crouch to enter, but beyond this final low passage lies the main chamber—the "Hall of Judgment," the chamber of the "open tomb." It is with respect and true humility that you make this final passage through the veil of tribulation and humility.

Once inside the Hall of Judgment, you are initiated into what must be a grand club of joyous, evolved Egos. You have earned, by your own efforts, this lofty position. At the far end of the chamber sits a huge, empty sarcophagus that signifies that the mystery we call death is no longer. The tomb is open, you are immortal.

Every key portion of the philosophy in the *Book of the Master* is embodied in stone within the Great Pyramid.

The allegories in stone and ancient literature match up and define a beautiful, individual philosophy. Yet even more remarkable is how these same allegories match the progress of civilization over the past 6,000 years.

CHAPTER SIX

Deciphering the Message

It makes no sense at all to build a structure as immense and as impressive as the Great Pyramid merely to convey to others in the future the fact that you, the builder, have knowledge of many scientific facts. The Great Pyramid is the most impressive edifice ever erected by man in order to ensure that when the purpose of its erection was finally discovered, the impact of that purpose would not easily be dismissed by the discoverers. The pyramid builders wanted to make sure we paid attention to their message, their "revelations in measures," when we finally began to get the significance of it all. Everything fits into place: the immense size, the precise construction, the geometric design, the allegorical meanings.

The process of deciphering the message, so that it makes unequivocal sense, has been a long, hard series of theory and controversy. After the men of science realized there was more to the proportions of the Great Pyramid than originally guessed, some unusual theories were advanced.

John Taylor, a London journalist who had never visited Egypt, opened the doors to decoding the pyramid's mathematical-astronomical message when he began to puzzle over the published dimensions of the monument. He was curious as to why the builders chose the 51 degree, 51 minute slope of angle rather than the standard equilateral triangle of 60 degrees. He made scale models of the structure and read everything he could find on it. Taylor concluded that the structure had been designed so that each face's area was equal to the square of the height.

It was Taylor who discovered the "pi" ratio embodied in the design, and to him it was too extraordinary to be attributed to chance. For thirty years Taylor worked with the geometry and geodesy of the Great Pyramid, and taking a page from the Frenchman Jomard's book, he wondered if the monument actually provided a measure of the earth. After forming this thesis, he began to search for a unit of measure that would properly fit. Toying with the number of the "pi" proportion, he was struck by the figure 366, which was very close to the number of days in the solar year. He also noted that the perimeter measure in inches (British inches) was exceedingly close to 36,600. He also noted that by dividing the base length by 25 inches he got a figure close to 366. He was musing over this curiosity—that a unit of measure so close could have been known to the pyramid builders—when Sir John Herschel postulated the polar-diameter inch.

Taylor saw the cold logic of the numbers, but

it was a well-known fact that the Egyptians of the Old Kingdom did not use any such units of measure. The two notions didn't mix. It isn't logical that the polar-diameter inch would be used by the Great Pyramid designer but not by the rest of the ancient Egyptians. Where else could the devoutly religious journalist turn for his answer but to the Old Testament?

An idea was born. Divine intervention provided the fantastic knowledge needed to design and build the Great Pyramid. The builders were members of the "chosen race," who later founded the monotheism of Israel; because the "pyramid inch" was so close to the British inch, the early inhabitants of the British Isles were related to the "lost tribes" of Israel. This is a thesis that cannot be disproved; however, it brought mostly derision from scholarly minds.

England at the time of Herschel and Taylor was being swept by the new philosophy of Darwinism. Charles Darwin had just published *The Origin of the Species*, which changed evolutionary thinking, and we can be sure the students of the day were more delighted to come from monkeys than from Puritans. Much like the social crises of our day, which blossomed from antiwar sentiments of "flower children"; England was in a tizzy. Bible fundamentalists were at a distinct disadvantage because blind faith and pulpit pounding can only attract a few from the mass of more "logical" thinkers. Darwin, though he had not intended it, had given antireligionists a scientific handle on an age-old argument, and they were gripping it and swinging the biological weapon with a vengeance against fundamentalism.

Those fundamentalists—who followed the dictates of Archbishop Usher, who argued that the world had been created in 4004 B.C. complete with fossils and geological evidences to confound mankind—needed a concrete handle on God and Revelations in order to grip the situation better and ward off the rapidly growing evolutionist concept.

And lo! "In the midst of the land of Egypt, the Lord had set signs and wonders even unto this day." Fundamentalists take the Bible literally, and there are definite references to the Great Pyramid in the Bible. The reasoning was astonishingly simple: the Egyptians could not have built the Great Pyramid since they lacked the intelligence, but God could have directed a few chosen people to do so. A few years later Taylor wrote, "The Great Pyramid, Why Was It Built and Who Built It?"—the Great Pyramid was being hailed by some erudite fanatics as "proof of God."

If we take the emotion out of the topic, which is usually impossible when religion is involved, we can readily see that such a Biblical hypothesis has more supporting evidence than the generally accepted tombic theory.

While America was embroiled in a civil war, John Taylor was corresponding with C. Piazzi Smyth, Astronomer Royal for Scotland and a good mathematician. Smyth did not deride the geometric reasoning put forth by Taylor, and when Taylor died, the determined Smyth sailed to Egypt to measure the Great Pyramid with greater accuracy than ever before, hoping to prove the builders used the "sacred cubit" of 25 pd-inches.

Smyth, too, became impressed with the precision of the geometry and astronomy obviously

The Great Pyramid of Cheops, at Giza. It is the first of the seven wonders of the ancient world and still a source of mystery and controversy. (UPI photo)

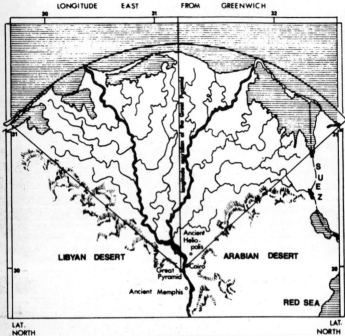

The entire Nile Delta is neatly encompassed by a quadrant set forth from the Great Pyramid. Some scholars believe this is what the Bible means when it refers to the pillar to the Lord in the center of Egypt and also at the border.

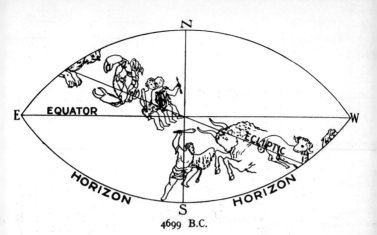

4699 B.C.

Dawning of the Age of Taurus. The pyramid's meridian projected at precisely midnight of the Autumnal Equinox 4700-4699 B.C. intersected the star marking the toe of Castor, one of the twins of Gemini. The ecliptic and celestial equator also intersected the same point, marking the movement of precession into the Zodiac sign of Taurus.

Celestial view from the Great Pyramid's meridian at midnight of the Autumnal equinox 4000-3999 B.C. Note the meridian, ecliptic and projected equator come together equidistant between the horns of Taurus. A full moon covered the same junction at the same time. This was clearly visible in the night sky. Invisible at noon of the Vernal equinox the same year. (See Chapter Eight.)

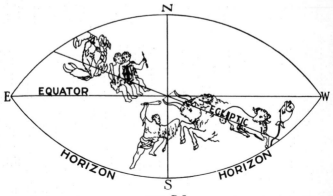

4000 B.C.

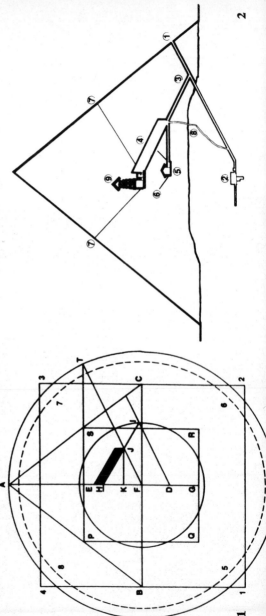

Diagram 1. The interior system of the Great Pyramid (see page 64) was built to monumentalize the geometry of the circle. The relationship between diameter and circumference is expressed as 3.14159, but it can be carried to infinity. The entire structural design of the Great Pyramid, including the interior passages and chambers, fits into this simple but fantastic geometric application, the only example of such design on earth today. *Diagram 2.* The interior system, by number: (1) Entrance passage on north face; (2) Subterranean chamber; (3) Ascending passage; (4) Grand Gallery; (5) Queen's Chamber; (6) Unfinished air shafts; (7) Air shafts; (8) Well shaft, tunneled in masonry rather than built; (9) King's chamber and antechamber. (See Chapter Five.)

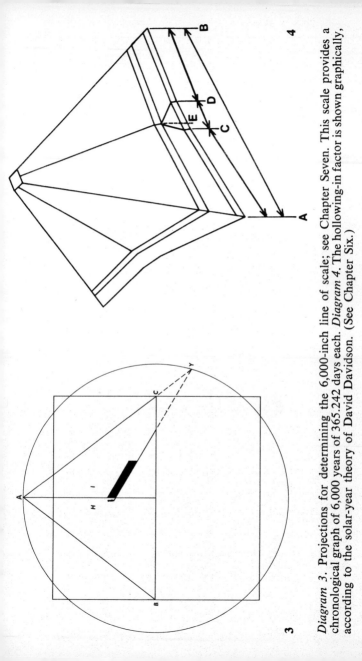

Diagram 3. Projections for determining the 6,000-inch line of scale; see Chapter Seven. This scale provides a chronological graph of 6,000 years of 365.242 days each. *Diagram 4.* The hollowing-in factor is shown graphically, according to the solar-year theory of David Davidson. (See Chapter Six.)

The Great Pyramid of Cheops, southwest corner, as viewed from the top of the Second Pyramid of Chephren. (UPI photo)

Author Tom Valentine at north base of the Great Pyramid. Unique slope of angle at this point is 51°-51′-14.3″ as shown by casing stone. *(Bottom)* Author begins exhausting climb up rugged face of the pyramid. Imagine this feat in terms of a 40-story building!

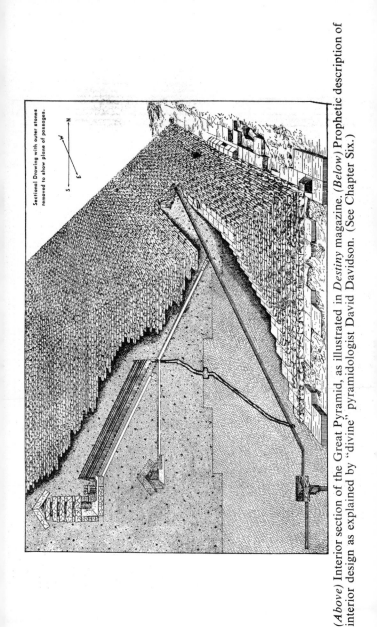

Sectional Drawing with outer stones removed to show plane of passages.

(*Above*) Interior section of the Great Pyramid, as illustrated in *Destiny* magazine. (*Below*) Prophetic description of interior design as explained by "divine" pyramidologist David Davidson. (See Chapter Six.)

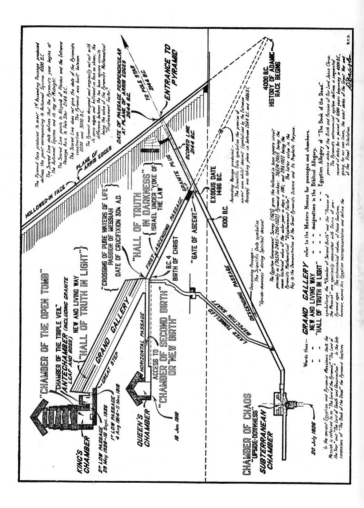

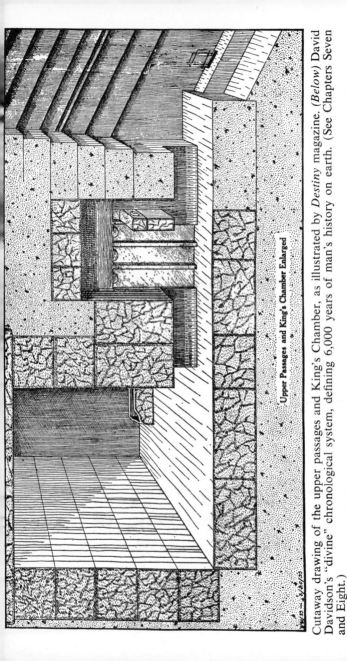

Upper Passages and King's Chamber Enlarged

Cutaway drawing of the upper passages and King's Chamber, as illustrated by *Destiny* magazine. *(Below)* David Davidson's "divine" chronological system, defining 6,000 years of man's history on earth. (See Chapters Seven and Eight.)

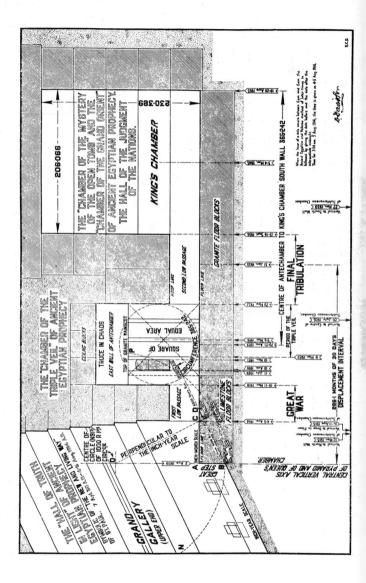

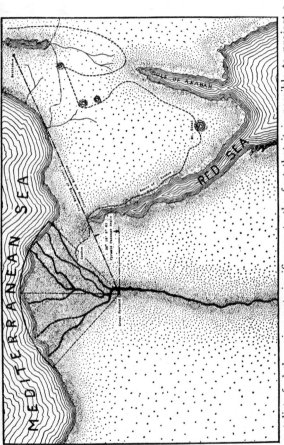

(*Above*) Fundamentalists feel there is great significance to the fact that it is possible to project a line from the Great Pyramid directly to Bethlehem, and have it pass through the area of the Red Sea where Moses parted the waters. The projected line is also the precise angle of the descending passage of the Great Pyramid. Illustrations from *Destiny* magazine. (*Below*) In the foreground, the pyramid of one of Cheops' relatives, much smaller and inferior in every way to the Great Pyramid in background.

Pat Flanagan, a leading exponent of "Pyramid Power." He has studied, measured, and metered the various energy fields involved with the pyramid shape. Among his many experiments are those of purifying water with a pyramid grid, and *(below)* his pyramid generator for maintaining the freshness of food, and enhancing flavors. (See Appendix One.)

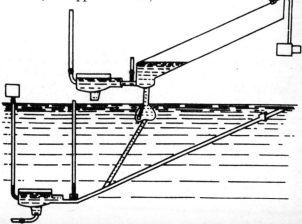

(Above) Precision-made Plexiglas scale model of pyramid as designed by the late John Dilley. These models are used in various experiments by schools and institutions. Reportedly, razor blades can be sharpened by the interior power of the "pyramid effect." Dehydration and mummification results are also reported! *(Below)* Sketch of Edward J. Kunkle's "Pharoah's Pump," U.S. Patent 2887956; a practical theory for the hydraulic engineering process possibly used in building the Great Pyramid. (See Appendix One.)

The Great Seal of the United States...a prophetic message?
A mystical reminder? The Latin phrase at the top translates
into "He has looked with favor on our beginning." The bottom
phrase translates into "The new order of the ages."

known to the builders, and he published his findings. His second book, *Our Inheritance in the Great Pyramid,* caused a great deal of controversy. Like Taylor, Smyth could find no rationale for attributing to the ancient Egyptians the knowledge for building the Great Pyramid, so he turned to the Bible.

His academic colleagues crucified him. Smyth was called the world's greatest "pyramidiot," and controversy raged. Then a man named Robert Menzies, another zealot, advanced a theory that the system of passages and chambers was nothing more than a chronological graph revealing prophecy. This made matters worse for Smyth.

Sir Flinders Petrie, the father of modern archeology, set out to measure the Great Pyramid's exterior with accuracy and to test the thesis put forth by Smyth. Petrie was amazed at the precision of the Great Pyramid's construction also, but after his detailed efforts, he concluded that Smyth's theory that the "sacred cubit" was the unit of measure used by the pyramid builders was in error. It was a scientific refutation, and it nearly killed any chances of serious consideration for Smyth's theories. Peter Tompkins in his *Secrets of the Great Pyramid* summed it up well: "In the conflict of opinions between biblical scholars and men of science, the true purpose of the Great Pyramid was buried in a rubble of verbiage."

The notion that the Great Pyramid's exterior measure was founded upon functions of the earth and its orbit around the sun and that it accurately incorporated the days of the solar year might have died with Taylor and Smyth had not a quiet genius named David Davidson come along with a resolve to *disprove* the "idiotic" theories of Robert Menzies, who said the Great Pyramid was "prophecy in stone."

Davidson was a structural engineer, architect, astronomer, mathematician, historian, and sober agnostic. If God existed, He certainly didn't go around whispering in ears how to build a pyramid filled with prophecy! Davidson spent twenty-five years studying the Great Pyramid. He blueprinted every stone of its interior system and reconstructed the monument, taking into account subsidence and earthquake damage. He attacked the data used by Menzies and other fanatics—and the more he dug into it, the more he was forced to accept it. In the end, this agnostic co-authored a massive volume entitled *The Great Pyramid—Its Divine Message*. No other book on the Great Pyramid is so extensive, so thorough, so analytical—and so hard to read.

Davidson explained how Smyth's base length, which fitted the number of days in a solar year, was accurate, despite the equally accurate survey by Petrie. He stressed that Petrie had noted the hollowing-in feature of the Great Pyramid's faces —something absolutely not present in the other pyramids—but had failed to extend this factor to the missing casing stones. Had he done so, he would have found that the base length matched Smyth's cubit to practical perfection.

Davidson's studies also took away any chance whatsoever that such a year-measure was "coincidental." That the perimeter of the Great Pyramid measured 36,524.22 pd-inches, therefore each side measured 365.242 sacred cubits, *could* be coincidence. It was unlikely, but possible.

Davidson demonstrated that the hollowing-in of each face was done in such a way as to embody all three "years" as they are represented by the earth's orbit. In Diagram Four (see page five of insert), the straight line, AB, measures 365.242 sacred cubits, which is also the precise number of days in the solar year. The solar year is determined by observing the exact time between two successive vernal or autumnal equinoxes. Line AC-DB accounts for the hollowing-in factor at the base, and it measures 365.256 sacred cubits, or precisely the number of days in a sideral or star-time year. This year is determined by the length of time it takes the earth to orbit the sun in relation to a fixed star. The difference of about twenty minutes each year is caused by the earth's axial wobble, which is responsible for the phenomenon of precession. Line AE-EB takes into account the slight difference between the hollowing-in factor at the base and at its deepest point of penetration into the core a few feet above the base; this measures 365.259 cubits, which is a fraction of a cubit or only about four minutes of time per year longer than the sideral year. This figure is precisely the number of days in the anomalistic year, which is figured by the amount of time it takes for the earth to travel from perihelion (closest point to the sun) back around to perihelion.

It's certain that the embodiment of all three known sources for determining the year is no accident.

Davidson's greatest discovery, however, was the figure he called the "displacement factor." This armed the engineer-astronomer with a distance he later used to overcome a discrepancy in the actual base measurement of the Great Pyramid. When the British government financed a survey of the Great Pyramid in 1925, Davidson was prepared for what they would determine to be the exact exterior measurement from corner to corner.

Davidson painstakingly demonstrated that the "Egyptian Chronological Lists," which were utilized by ancient Egyptian priesthoods to rationalize the ascensions to the throne and the national heritage, literally outlined the Great Pyramid's "intended" dimensions in pd-inches. He proved that the various "King's lists" used to chronicle the passage of generations added up to a total of 36,524 years. Since the ancient Egyptian Chronicles are not necessary to the thesis of the Great Pyramid's purpose, I will not go into the matter in detail.

In his preface to the third edition of *The Great Pyramid—Its Divine Message*, which he wrote with the help of Bible scholar H. Aldersmith, Davidson writes:

> The Great Pyramid's Displacement Factor is the fundamental mathematical value that explains the purpose of the scientific Pyramid dimensions appearing in the ancient Egyptian Chronological List, and that merges all these scientific dimensions into the common theme of the design. The Pyramid dimensions of the Egyptian Chronological Lists agree —with a single exception only—with the existing indications of measurements for the Great Pyramid, as these have been derived from Sir Flinders Petrie's accurate survey. The single exception is Sir Flinders Petrie's own *reconstruction* of the Pyramid's square base. By projecting the lines of the existing casing

base edges, where these were found near the center of each base side, he obtained the positions of what he believes to have been the original base corners. The resulting square base circuit is less than the square base circuit of the Egyptian lists by the value of the Great Pyramid's Displacement Factor.

Davidson went on to stress that the clearing away of debris around the Great Pyramid's base, taking place as he was writing the preface, would show "definitely that the builders did not carry out the precise intentions of the designer." Since the builders did not carry out the designer's intention in this respect, Davidson demonstrated that it was part of the Pyramid's structural and scientific allegory that this error of "the builders" should be thus monumentalized to make "the structural allegory agree perfectly with the scriptural allegory, and confirm it in every respect."

In his lectures Davidson explained that the actual physical measurement from corner to corner would fall short of the "perfect" Egyptian list dimension by about 24 feet, or precisely 286.1022 pd-inches—the figure he called the Displacement Factor. When the survey was actually announced, Davidson showed that the actual perimeter in pd-inches was 36,238.15. By adding the factor of 286.1022, we have a sum of 36,524.25 or the "designers'" figure to a hundredth of an inch. Davidson had been able to correctly predict that precise difference between the actual construction and the geometrically perfect design because the Displacement Factor is exceptionally scientific.

Let's look at how this factor of 286.1022 pd-inches is embodied in the structure. First, the interior passage system is offset to the left of the north-south axis of the Great Pyramid by exactly 286.1022 pd-inches. The center of the King's Chamber is offset from the east-west axis of the monument by exactly 286.1022 pd-inches. Davidson claimed the missing apex was short from the projected point by exactly 286.1022 pd-inches. The precise difference in the height of the ascending passage and the height of the Grand Gallery is 286.1022 pd-inches. The figure is repeatedly and deliberately embodied in the design and construction of the Great Pyramid. It is an amazing number, and Davidson points out that it has many scientific uses—from determining the rate of precession to a theory of relativity.

Davidson believed the factor symbolized the difference between nature's perfection and man's will. He felt that man was "displaced" from perfection, or God, by that precise factor, just as the exterior of the Pyramid was displaced from perfection by that factor.

Davidson didn't think of this one, but I'm willing to bet that if the optimum duration of the human gestation period could be determined with exactness, it would be 286 days. The Great Pyramid's Displacement Factor is a factor to be reckoned with, and much science of the future will utilize it.

What David Davidson accomplished was to incorporate so much exacting science and math into the controversy regarding the purpose of the Great Pyramid that the arguments from detractors degenerated to name-calling and character assassination, thus avoiding the factual issues.

To fully understand the scientific message, we

need to explore some basic astronomy—which is neatly embodied in the Great Pyramid.

The phenomenon of "precession" is caused by the earth's wobble, but we don't really know what causes the wobble itself. As the earth spins, the wobble causes an apparent movement of the stars. The complete circuit of this movement takes approximately 26,000 years or one "Great Year." Astrologers have divided the Great Year into twelve segments, one for each sign of the Zodiac, and they call the period of time that it takes to pass through each sign an "age." This is about 2,100 years. We're familiar with the "Age of Aquarius" that is supposedly upon us—the Great Pyramid covers this topic too, as we shall see.

The precise number of years in the cycle of precession varies because the rate of precession isn't uniform. The sum of the base diagonals of the Great Pyramid is 25,826.5 pd-inches, and that just happens to be exactly the number of years calculated for the total circuit of precession. It's amazing to note that the perimeter measurement of the Great Pyramid at the thirty-fifth course of masonry, which is a course constructed at a greater width than the others, also equals the "precessional circuit" of 25,826.5 years.

People have been so boggled by the prospects of all these year-cycle proportions and measurements that they have argued against the chances of their being true on the sheer weight of the odds alone. This is unrealistic. It's obvious that the universe is one of order and precision—the Great Pyramid builders have simply monumentalized that order and precision in the stone structure, by boiling everything down to gravitational astronomy and factors taken directly from the earth and its orbit. The year-circle gives us a pyramid whose base diagonals match the great year of precession. The structure in turn embodies the universal geometric relationship of "pi." It's amazingly simple, neat, and enchanting. No wonder Pythagoras, who studied in Egypt, boiled the universe down to geometry and numbers.

Davidson showed that the ancient pyramid builders, whom he believed to have been divinely inspired, use a

> system of geometry in a graphical demonstration of Natural Law, defining the linear and angular measurements of the earth and its orbit; defining the annual rates and periods of the cyclical motions of the earth and its orbit; and defining a system of astronomical chronology that can be the basis of related reference for every period or highly developed stage of civilization in the world's history.
>
> With these items established as identities, the identities became intentional identities. With the latter established, there will be proved that a former civilization was more highly skilled in the science of gravitational astronomy—and therefore in the mathematical basis of the mechanical arts and sciences—than modern civilization. And what will this mean? It will mean that it has taken man thousands of years to discover by experiment facts he had originally come to know by another surer and simpler method. It will mean, in effect, that the whole empirical basis of modern civilization is a makeshift collection of hypotheses compared with the Natural Law of the civilization of the past.

Which "civilization of the past" is Davidson referring to? Certainly not that of the ancient Egyptians. Davidson was also forced to go to

Divine Inspiration as the source for the intelligence to build the Great Pyramid because he rejected the notion of Atlantis and Lemuria. The years of study converted the great scientist from a sober agnostic to a deeply religious man who came to believe that the British were part of the "chosen people" and the pyramid inch helped prove it. His personal beliefs then became the issue, and his science was ignored. Critics ripped his religious conviction and sidestepped the facts embodied in the Great Pyramid. In some matters where interpretation was necessary, Davidson erred; he allowed his beliefs to color his logic. Davidson's interpretations, however, are one thing; the science of the Great Pyramid is quite another. He showed the way to deciphering the significance of all this monumentalized precision; he found the key that unlocked what he called a "Divine Message."

CHAPTER SEVEN

Instrument of Prophecy

In 1964, John A. Wilson published a book titled *Signs and Wonders Upon Pharaoh*. It is an interesting account of the many individuals who make up the panorama of Egyptology and archeological exploration in that ancient land. Typical of orthodox Egyptology, Wilson dismisses the largest portion of the Great Pyramid's science, and hangs the "blame" for what he considers "lunatic pyramidology" on poor old Piazzi Smyth. I quote from Wilson's book:

> A very different person was Piazzi Smyth. By definition he was a scholar, since he was Professor of Astronomy at Edinburgh and the Astronomer Royal of Scotland. He became a crackpot whose weird ideas still leave a troublesome legacy to the Egyptologist. Working first at home and using the figures of others, and then surveying the Great Pyramid himself in 1865, he came to some fantastic conclusions. In effect, they implied that the ancient

Egyptians had a mathematical knowledge and an engineering skill far beyond any people up to modern times. He found the mathematical value "pi" present in the construction of the Great Pyramid. He worked out to his own satisfaction a unit of measurement and architecture for the Great Pyramid, which he called the "pyramid inch" equal to 1.001 of our inches. For him the empty sarcophagus in the King's Chamber was unimportant as a place of burial because he believed that it had been designed as a standard measure of capacity for all people in all times.

This could be dismissed as unimportant lunacy, if there were not good people today who believe that the ancient Egyptians had some powerful and lost knowledge, believing particularly that the Great Pyramid was designed by God as an instrument of prophecy.

In his book of some 70,000 words, Wilson has devoted three cursory paragraphs to the subject of the Great Pyramid's scientific mystique. He offers not a single scrap of evidence to refute that such a mystique exists, but he heaps scathing criticism upon Smyth. And he did so, obviously ignorant of many of the facts that have already been presented regarding the theories of the polar-diameter inch and the year-circle. Wilson ascribes to the tombic theory, and he wrote a good book about orthodox Egyptology—I am using his example only as a means to show the "normal" reaction to any idea that the Great Pyramid could possibly be an "instrument of prophecy."

Every time the notion of prophecy and the Great Pyramid pops into a conversation with anyone who has some knowledge of Egyptology, there is immediately an air of intellectual snobbery. "How could anyone think such a thing possible? It's sheer nonsense."

Invariably, the detractor making such a statement knows about as much regarding the Great Pyramid as he could have obtained from reading Wilson's book.

Since there is no writing anywhere inside the Great Pyramid, how can it contain prophecy? The answer is, by using science, stone, and allegory in such a way as to avoid all the problems of language—problems of translation, interpretation, and semantics.

To establish this remarkable "revelation in measure," we will stick with these scientific constants:

1. The polar-diameter inch and its obvious relation to the solar year. One pd-inch equals 365.242 days.

2. The stone construction as it exists and can be measured. We will not dislodge and move any of the stones that have been in place for 6,500 years in order to meet any criteria; nor will we file down any parts of the stones to match our thesis.

3. The consistent allegory found in the ancient *Book of the Master* will always apply to the chambers and passages.

4. Our starting point will be determined by the exacting sciences of geometry and astronomy.

In order to make a chronological graph, we must first have a straight line with logical beginning and ending points. To determine the length of the straight line, we resort to the geometry of the Great Pyramid and its relationship to astronomy. Davidson clearly demonstrated that the geometry of the interior links the pd-inch and the solar year; furthermore, astronomy and the pyramid geometry limit the length of time to be covered by the inch-year graph to no more than one-fourth the period of precession, or approximately 6,500 years.

Within the Great Pyramid's interior system, there is not a single straight line covering a length of 6,000 pd-inches, let alone 6,500. However, referring to Diagram Three (see insert), which gives the geometry of the year-cycle as the basis for the pyramid's interior design, let's extend the analogy and geometry. Extend line AC to the year-circle's circumference at Y. Extend line HI to the year-circle circumference, and you'll see it also joins at Y. In actuality we have projected the arris edge of the Great Pyramid beneath the surface rock to a point where it is joined by a projection of the floor line of the ascending passage. The distance from that juncture up the sloping angle to the only physical marker in the entire structure measures precisely 6,000 pd-inches, not a hair off.

Thus we have described a straight line on which our chronological graph can be placed—an inch-year scale covering 6,000 inches; 6,000 years of 365.242 days each. Now all we need is a starting time, and we'll have a time—distance scale.

Davidson and other fundamentalists arbitrarily chose the year 4000 B.C., because this was their idea of when the "Adamic" race was started. It is an arbitrary starting point. However, there is scientific proof that the starting point is almost exactly that date. Astronomy and the pyramid combine to indicate the starting point is precisely 3999 B.C. at midnight of the autumnal equinox (September 22). This is getting so exact it's disturbing.

The entrance passage of the Great Pyramid descends according to geometric calculations—it also descends in line with a certain star that becomes the northern pole star on a cyclical basis of about 1,290 years. This is the star designated as *Alpha Draconis*. Davidson painstakingly worked star charts backward in time to determine the precise position of this star in relation to the Great Pyramid's entrance passage. He determined that *Alpha Draconis* shined directly down the passage for a period of a few years at precisely midnight of the autumnal equinox. The median year was 2144 B.C. Smyth had calculated the date to be about 2141 B.C.

About thirty feet down the entrance passage there are two unusual joints that call attention to a double-scored line marking all four walls. The double-scored lines indicate right angles from the slope of passage rather than right angles to sea level. Smyth and Menzies felt this was an obvious marker. Davidson, when attacking the idea as "silly," finally calculated that this marker pointed directly to an important star—Alcyone in the constellation Pleiades—at exactly the same time, midnight, autumnal equinox, 2144 B.C.

Due to precession the two stars will come together at that singular spot on the face of the earth only briefly during the 25,286.5 years of the cycle. The marked date thus offers confirmation for a starting date of the inch-year scale. Measuring down the passage and then projecting the measure down the scale, we can determine the starting date to be 3999 B.C. This means that 6,000 years later the timeline ends—A.D. 2001, a scant twenty-six years hence.

Inch by inch, year by year, the timeline moves

upward from the starting date. There is nothing to catch our attention moving up the projected portion of the line, but finally we reach the juncture of the descending passage and the Gate of Ascent. The date we obtain from our chronograph is 1486 B.C.

Davidson and Aldersmith went to great lengths to prove that this is the exact date of the Exodus, but this is one of the areas where Davidson allowed his beliefs to color his logic. It could possibly be the date when Moses was born, providing he was about 130 years old at the time of the Exodus. Since our knowledge of history is limited, we cannot determine what took place in 1486 B.C. that could have had a major effect on Western Civilization. We can simply note the date on our chronograph and continue onward and upward.

The end of the granite plug would mark our scale at about 1350 B.C., which perhaps coincides with the estimated time of Exodus—but again we can only surmise.

According to the analogy from the *Book of the Master*, after these particular dates, civilization, like each aspiring individual, was moving up the Hall of Truth in Darkness.

The next juncture we have is the precise point where the floor level of the Chamber of Second Birth, or New Birth, strikes a perpendicular to our chronograph. It is interesting to return to the description of the entrance corridor to the Queen's Chamber, or the Chamber of New Birth. The floor level suddenly "drops" a couple of feet, without apparent reason. Now we can find a remarkable reason. Projecting the floor line of the chamber over to the ascending passage, the juncture will strike our time-distance scale or chronograph at the date—October 4, 4 B.C. The "new birth" marks the precise birthdate of Jesus Christ, whose life and work have affected this planet more profoundly than any other Ego in historic memory.

The first thing most people think is "Wasn't Christ born on zero A.D.?" Actually, when Dionysius Exiguus was calculating the Gregorian calendar we use today, he figured that the birth of Christ took place in the twenty-eighth year of the reign of Augustus Caesar. However, he overlooked the fact that Augustus had ruled Rome for four years under his true name, Octavian. Therefore Dionysius made a four-year mistake. That Christ was born in October, especially on October 4, can be debated, but this is the date given by the Great Pyramid, and Davidson and Aldersmith went to great lengths to prove it.

It is, if it wasn't intentional as orthodoxy will have us believe, the most amazing coincidence of all that exacty 33½ pd-inches further up our chronograph, the narrow Hall of Truth in Darkness opens brilliantly into the Grand Gallery, or the Hall of Truth in Light. The precise date on our timeline for the Crucifixion was April 6, A.D. 30. Davidson once again let his beliefs cloud his science, and he juggled the date a little in his lectures to be April 7, A.D. 30, because April 6 would have been a Thursday and "everybody knows" Christ was crucified on Good Friday. The Pyramid knows best, however. In 1973, a professor from the University of Tennessee used a computer and worked moon cycles back in time to determine that the Crucifixion actually took place on Thursday, April 6, A.D. 30.

What an amazing bit of forecasting! Some ancient elders knew the precise date these momentous occasions in the history of Western civilization occurred—and they knew them at least 4,700 years before they happened. There's a message in that bit of fact, to be sure.

What a magnificent way to forecast the occasion. A narrow, dark passage, labeled the Hall of Truth in Darkness, suddenly becomes a huge, two-story gallery of unmatched architecture at precisely the point the greatest Teacher in history died on a cross.

Despite the marvel, the science, and the truth of it all—does it seem logical that human beings put perhaps eighty years of effort into the construction of a monument to tell us something we already knew and were affected by? No, there's more, much more.

The prophetic chronograph continues up the floor line of the Grand Gallery until it reaches the foot of the great step. The date is 1844, and we are at a loss for historic significance. The Baha'i faith could claim it if they so desired; that year is significant in their history. The angular ascending line continues upward until it strikes the center of the granite slab in the antechamber, 6,000 inch-years from the starting point. What will be the significance of A.D. 2001? Other than that it was a great name for a movie, many people believe this millennium marker will usher in the "new age," the "Kingdom of God." Because that is a nice, positive thing to believe, I too think the year 2001 will usher in a new, virtuous civilization that enables mankind to accelerate its spiritual and egoic growth.

We have seen that without a single inscription, but using geometry, astronomy, stone construction, and allegory from ancient literature, we have named two extremely important dates in our culture. However, it is like a roadmap through time—the 6,000 inch-year line is on one side of the map. Turn the map over to get a closer view of a particular area, and you'll find that nothing's changed in the description of the countryside, except the distance scale. No longer does an inch equal fifty miles, an inch now equals three miles.

The Great Pyramid builders used the same principle to telescope the all-important twentieth century for clear viewing. Once atop the great step, we are standing on the "Floor of the Temple" facing the "Chamber of the Triple Veil." According to the *Book of the Master*, when "Osiris walked on the floor of the temple, each marker was for 30 days." The only marker we know of is the pd-inch. We are changing our scale. Instead of 365.242 days as it was over the 6,000-inch line, the pd-inch now equals thirty days as we "walk on the floor of the temple." The present century is outlined in the Great Pyramid by a special chronology. If this is truth, then history should prove it. It does.

From the foot of the great step, which coincides on the original inch-year chronograph to January 1844, to the top of the great step, we obtain a starting time for the special chronology—August 2, 1909. From that point and that date forward—without juggling the time or distance—we count each pd-inch as thirty days.

The stones of the Chamber of the Triple Veil have been in place for nearly 6,500 years. The measurements of the chambers have been taken over and over again by exceptionally careful scholars. Our scientific constants hold—the inch is still one-five hundred millionth the polar diameter of the earth; the *Book of the Master* is still our allegorical authority; the actual construction remains unchanged, and our starting point has been taken off the original scale, which was determined by geometry and astronomy.

The first veil, you may recall, is conflict. The perpendicular struck by the stone marking the beginning of that first veil strikes our floor chronograph at a point marking the date August 5, 1914.

The perpendicular struck by the other end of the stone marking "conflict" marks our timeline at the date November 11, 1918. The veil of conflict is thus outlined to occur between August 5, 1914, and November 11, 1918.

Early on the morning of August 5, 1914, Great Britain declared war on Germany, and World War I was truly a world war. On November 11, 1918, the armistice was declared. How specific can prophecy be?

The period of "truce in chaos" extended from November 11, 1918, until May 29, 1928. On the latter date the granite block marking the beginning of the final veil, which is "tribulation and humility," strikes our scale. The "tribulation" of our Western world is evidently economic. We will understand "humility" when our economic system crumbles despite our efforts to save it. Of course, this is only conjecture, but the commodity prices on the London market began to decline on May 29, 1928. The battle of the gold standard began at that time, and the value of the pound sterling declined. The surest sign of a civilization's decline is the devaluation of its money. Our civilization has not regained the "gold" standard.

The end of the veil is marked by the entrance into the Hall of the Judgment. The date on our chronograph is September 16, 1936. I understand that in Chicago during the early 1930s a David Davidson society was formed. These prophetic dates had already been outlined by Davidson's book years before, so followers were anticipating the worst when the "world plunged into the Hall of Judgment." These followers were part of a growing group professing "Anglo-Israelism," and they caught the fancy of some of the news media.

The following is taken from the *Literary Digest* of September 26, 1936, ten days after our civilization marched into the Hall of Judgment.

Where were you at noon on September 16? Remember it well; it may have been the end of the world or the beginning of a new era.

For almost a hundred years, prophets, astrologers, students of the pyramids and sundry religious seers have proclaimed this an hour of importance, at which anything might happen. There may have been some minor quibbling over the exact moment because of daylight saving, but all agreed that, by midday, the worst or the best would have come and gone.

Perhaps something untoward did happen. Only the seers, the pyramids, the stars, the Sphinx and a mysterious Mr. 666 know.

In Egypt the Great Pyramid of Cheops, cause of all the excitement, was the cynosure of prophetic eyes. Three hundred feet distance, the Sphinx (symbol of silence) with woman's head, bull's body, lion's claws and eagle's wings, ran true to form. Guarding the pyramids, she said nothing.

According to "pyramidologists," every inch of

Cheops' main interior route means something. Armed with tape measures, note-books and rulers they have long been convinced of the secret and occult significance in the structure and measurements of the Great Pyramid. From one end to the other, the various passageways and chambers are supposed to symbolize the years from 2625 B.C. to 2001 A.D. After that the builders seemed to run out of space and sense of time.

The fanciest measuring inside the Egyptian monument has brought the world to the King's Chamber. After a long, hard trek up the low passage from May 28, 1928, one is now able to stand erect again.

There are some 200,000 avid "pyramidologists" notably in England. Sooner or later, their prophecies get tied up with the future of Anglo-Saxon races. Now that the troublesome sixteenth is past, they are inspecting the next developments of their rulers. For seventeen years, fateful events, reshaping the human race, will lead up to the Armageddon of 1953. During this time, the Anglo-Saxon races will restore Israel to Palestine. Then the age of turbulence will cease. From 1953 until the final slumber in 2001, every one will breathe easier, just sitting around and speculating on the next move. But the pyramid won't be of any use then, as it will have run out of inches.

Regardless of what did or didn't happen on September 16, the students are proud of their measured prophecies. The only vexing miscalculation made so far was for the signing of the armistice. They are fourteen hours of inches out, but this was explained away as identical with the abdication and flight of the Kaiser to Holland.

Taking these forays into the past of Egyptian architecture as groundwork, hard working prophets, amateur and professional, made much of the 1936 Ides of September. White-haired Edna Bandler appeared in New York in flowing white robe and veil. Warning all of the world shaking events at hand, she called newspaper men "rascals"; preachers

112

"false prophets"; and scientists direct descendants of Lucifer, the light-bearer.

Denouncing the world, she declared people were now to receive their sixty-eighth dispensation. "There will be no further period of grace," she warned. "Now the rule will be by iron. Those who sin will pay for it on the spot."

In New Jersey, a religious sect, the Assembly, went on its knees to pray for deliverance, three days before the fatal moment. The leader, Robert J. Boyle, wasn't sure what was going to happen, but he hinted it was high time for the antichrist, Mr. 666, to appear. To his way of thinking, several modern dictators might easily fit the role.

The journalist who penned that commentary was witty, and his column was enjoyable reading, despite his obvious lack of thorough understanding of pyramidology. For example, the armistice is not erroneously dated by the chronology derived from geometry and astronomy according to David Davidson. Anyway, hindsight is always easier than foresight. The kooks that took the September 16, 1936, date to mean the end of the world got everything they deserved if they shot their mouth off. In Chicago there was a sudden decrease in the David Davidson Society membership lists, and eventually the organization folded.

There are always a few who interpret strangely and perhaps act wrongly in carrying out their beliefs. And there are always many more who will jeer when the "abnormal" belief proves erroneous. But it would be a monumental mistake for us today to take the witticism of a magazine journalist to heart and allow it to cause us to overlook the entire message in the Great Pyramid.

It is unfortunate that Davidson became caught

up in the notion of Anglo-Israelism. This particular view has a strong tendency to turn people off, especially non-Anglo-Saxons. An interesting commentary on the Anglo-Israelism views was printed by *The Christian Century* magazine shortly after the September 16 date everyone learned in pyramidology had awaited.

A letter was sent in to a feature called "The Question Box," as follows:

> I have seen the statement that the Great Pyramid of Egypt contains in its measurements and inscriptions certain predictions covering the centuries since its construction, indicating the chief events in the history of the world and the beginning of a crisis in human affairs to be ushered in about the middle of this month of September, 1936. What are the facts?

The answer, supplied by a writer with the initials H.L.W. read:

> It is the contention of those who profess the theory known as Anglo-Israelism that the Anglo-Saxon race is the surviving representative of the "Ten Lost Tribes" of Hebrew history who were supposed to have migrated westward and settled in Ireland, becoming the ancestors of the British and American peoples. Similar is the belief of the so-called "Messengers of Jehovah," a group organized by Pastor Russell of Brooklyn, and carried on by Judge Rutherford of Pasadena, California. The theory, which has been exploited in both Great Britain and on this continent rests upon extremely literal interpretations of scripture, and fantastic guesses regarding the fulfillment of "prophecies" and is devoid of any scientific basis.
>
> A pendant of this theory is the belief that the Great Pyramid of Egypt is an ancient embodiment

of forecasts of the future from the age of its construction, under Khufu in the fourth millennium B.C. to the end of time. These conjectures are based upon measurements of the outer dimensions and the inner passages of the pyramid—a cubit to a year, the cubit employed being not the measure used by the Egyptians, the Hebrews or any other known people, but a so-called "pyramid cubit" whose employment is made to fit the requirements of the speculation. There are no inscriptions within or outside the pyramid. A considerable literature has grown up around the assumption, setting forth the discovery of dates, some important and some insignificant, indicated by the direction and dimensions of the mortuary passages within the structure. The thesis is a remarkable example of elaborate and painstaking adaptation of structural facts to meet the requirements of theory which has no foundation either in history or in scripture. . . .

Once again we see the author of an influential publication showing his lack of solid information about "pyramidology."

There is no doubt that many volumes of tripe have been written and many notions of pure chicanery have been forwarded under the guise of pyramidology—but we cannot allow reality to be colored by the misrepresentations of others in times past.

The idea that the original Anglo-Saxons were part of the "Ten Lost Tribes" stems mainly from the link between the British inch and the pd-inch. Undoubtedly, it was used by peoples who designed Stonehenge, whose inner circle has a precise diameter of 3,652.42 pd-inches. This circular area would fit perfectly into one quarter of the base of the Great Pyramid—that unit of measure was indeed used by the ancient Egyptians. They called it

115

a quarter-aroura—four of them make up the thirteen-acre base square of the Great Pyramid. Thus we can see the Egyptians inherited a little of the Hykso system.

The Anglo-Israelists make an interesting conjecture from the prophecy of Daniel. When Daniel was being taken out of Jerusalem and enslaved by Nebuchadnezzar, the year was 603 B.C. By interpreting a dream, he prophesied that this was the beginning of a long time of exile for the Jews from their capital city. According to Anglo-Israelists, he said the gentiles would hold Jerusalem for seven cycles—these were periods of 360 years each, one for every degree in a circle. Then, at the beginning of the seventh cycle, the great "stone race" would rise up to rule the world, and at the end of the seventh cycle this stone race would release Jerusalem from the gentiles and give it back to the Jews. Starting from 603 B.C., we find the seventh cycle beginning in 1557–1558, December–January. That is precisely when Queen Elizabeth I took charge and England became virtual master of the world. Exactly 360 years later, December 1917, General Allenby marched his army into Jerusalem and rid it of the Turks. The rest is history—Jerusalem had been returned to the Jews by the British, as this group claims was prophesied.

Although that is an extremely accurate prophecy and the inch relationship is obvious, these are extremely weak points on which to make claims for the Anglo-Saxons being part of the "lost" tribes and therefore somehow to be put in charge of the world during the time of "Judgment."

September 16, 1936, wasn't a very monumental day as far as historic activity is concerned. I checked the papers and learned that Sarah Churchill ran off with an actor on that date.

However, there are many people who believe that that date in the Great Pyramid's special chronology coincides with the "sounding of the Seventh Trumpet" from the book of Revelation. It is a date that is suposed to have marked the beginning of the "times of the end." Chances are we won't know the significance of that date unless the rest of the prophecy is accurate and a "New Order of the Ages" is started after 2001.

The next clear-cut perpendicular to the inch–thirty-day scale is where we run out of room against the south wall of the King's Chamber. At this point we must make a turn—a 90-degree turn —in order to continue onward. The date is August 20, 1953, and other than it being my eighteenth birthday, not much of significance happened. It has been pointed out that this was the day Russian scientists exploded the H-bomb for the first time. I'm not impressed with that event; the pyramid deals in far bigger things.

On August 20, 1953, we entered the "Age of Aquarius, according to Great Pyramid reckoning —and that's an event to be reckoned with.

CHAPTER EIGHT

The Age of Enlightenment

For the past two decades we have been hearing rumblings and rumors about the Age of Aquarius. We are, according to astrologers, approaching a time when we will be immersed in this "new age" and profound changes will take place. Further, we often hear it said that "the Age of Aquarius is an era of enlightenment."

The Great Pyramid, unlike astrologers, states unequivocally in geometry and stone that the Age of Aquarius has dawned—on August 20, 1953. In conjunction with this, as more and more people find a new awareness of history and humanity—such as we can find by studying the mysteries of the Great Pyramid—we may indeed demonstrate that we are entering an age of enlightenment.

Astrology is an interesting art. I have been amazed and impressed by some astrologers whose accuracy in reading aspects of my character and behavior was truly phenomenal. On the other hand, I have developed disdain for the "sun sign" gibberish we find in the daily newspapers. It is ironic that most newspaper editors hate to waste the space with useless horoscope verbiage that they believe readers demand. Few, if any, of these editors have really investigated the subject in order to learn they are printing the worst possible aspect of it. The general attitude toward astrology is very much like the general attitude toward pyramidology—sneeringly skeptical, with a solid foundation in ignorance.

Astrologers insist that their art is a science. And perhaps they use enough math and astronomy to. feel that way, but astrology is interpretive and therefore too subjective to be truly classified scientific. I would say they are about as scientific as psychologists—and they have about as many schools of thought as psychologists do.

There is one danger inherent in astrology that I want to relate before getting back to the subject at hand. This is the danger of placing limits on ability and free will because of something suggested by the position of the heavenly bodies. Every astrologer worth his salt urges people to use astrology only as a guideline for reason and common sense, and if conflict arises, go with reason and experience, not astrology.

Regardless of the controversy, one thing is certain—astrology has a definite effect on society.

Earlier we learned that the duration of an "age" is determined by the precessional circuit. An age is one-twelfth the circuit, or roughly 2,100 years. In the past year I have asked many of the better astrologers just exactly when this new age takes place. The answer is invariably vague. Most of them are agreed it is quite a while in the future, but none have named a precise date for the dawning of this new and wonderful age. One of the acknowledged experts admitted, "We don't really use astronomy as the basis for figuring the new age."

Astronomy is an exacting science. Ask an astronomer when we are going to enter the Age of Aquarius, and he will say that it's impossible to determine because there is no clear-cut cusp, or borderline, between the constellations of Pisces and Aquarius.

Remember, as our world turns, it wobbles, and this wobble causes the plane of the axis to pass slowly through the various constellations that encircle the ecliptic. The ecliptic is the path of our orbit around the sun, projected into space. A long time ago, someone drew pictures by number from star to star to give the clusters form or identity. The pictures in a ring around the ecliptic are callled the Zodiac. The rationale, then, is that eventually during the cycle of precession the plane of our axis will pass through each sign for the duration of an "age" defined by that sign. The problem, as the astronomer sees it, is that there is no borderline between Pisces and Aquarius; the two signs are pretty much intermingled.

Another problem, not generally recognized by astrologers who are unable to agree on the precise dawning of the new age, is the method of reckoning. There are two kinds of astronomical reckoning—diurnal and nocturnal. One is with the sun, the other anti-sun. Diurnal reckoning uses noon of the vernal equinox, or the first day of spring, as an annual beginning point. Nocturnal reckoning used midnight of the autumnal equinox for its beginning point. That's about as opposite as you can get. Oriental astrologers, I am told, use nocturnal reckoning and have done so for thousands of years. Western astrologers use diurnal reckoning.

Because an astrologer's analysis of my personal situation was so accurate, I assume the form of reckoning makes no difference in making up an individual chart. However, it makes a universe of difference when trying to calculate the dawning of a new age.

Because the Great Pyramid monumentalizes the date, I am convinced the dawning of this new age is significant. The date of August 20, 1953, is marked on the temple floor timeline by the juncture of the south wall of the chamber. We can go no further without making a 90-degree turn. What more lucid way could there be to signify a change in direction? The expression "times are changing" has never been truer. But what does the new age bring?

How can I be so sure that the date marks the beginning of the new age? Let's examine the reason for making this astronomical claim. The only place I've ever read that this was the meaning for the date was in the book that started it all for me, *The Ultimate Frontier*.

David Davidson does not make such a claim for the date, but it is from data in his huge tome that I found the necessary proofs. Davidson used the writings of Lockyer, Jensen, and Brown—three top authorities—to determine how much knowledge the ancient civilizations really had about precession, the Zodiac, and orbital movement.

The earliest astrologers are believed to have

been the Chaldeans of the pre-Babylon era. But, as we have already noted, it requires literally ages of trial-and-error peering into the night sky to come up with enough viable data to make calculations and interpretations. The ancients obviously inherited the basics of astronomy and astrology from people who carried such knowledge over from the previous civilizations.

Scholars of astrology know that the ancients used a different Zodiac than we use today. The pictures have remained the same, which is amazing, but the concept has changed. Anyone can see that the pictures drawn by number among the stars don't fit the degrees of a circle perfectly. For example, Taurus the bull is 40 degrees, and Aries the ram is 20 degrees. The original "pre-Chaldean" Zodiac was made up of *six* signs of 60 degrees each. Sir Norman Lockyer listed them as follows: "Taurus; Crab or Tortoise; Virgin, or ear of corn; Scorpion; Capricornis; and Pisces." This system was carried into Babylonian and Egyptian times, but it shared the rostrum with an independent and ancient system of unknown origin that featured the "balance," or Libra. This secondary system had twelve signs.

It is pertinent here to warn you that I am over-simplifying—to cover this in proper detail would require hundreds of pages.

Brown, in his book *Primitive Constellations*, points out that the "earliest possible" date in history for people to have been given, or have had to learn to use, "equinoctial years" featuring signs of the Zodiac would have been the year 4699 B.C. You may recall that earlier I surmised that the Hykso elders in charge of building the Great Pyramid smiled with delight when they observed the stars from atop their new structure, which did not yet have an apex stone. They smiled because as they looked into the universe above them, the meridian of their pyramid projected into the midnight sky passed through the star that marks the toe of Castor. The star that signifies the toe of Castor, one of the twins in the constellation Gemini, marks the dividing line between Taurus and Gemini. At midnight of the autumnal equinox in the year 4699 B.C., the stars were visible and the projected pyramid meridian at precisely midnight crossed the ecliptic and celestial equator at the exact same spot in the heavens. All three projected lines crossed in the toe of Castor. Astronomers have confirmed this fact by determining the present position of the toe of Castor and using Simon Newcomb's figures for the rate of precession. Incidentally, the formula for the rate of precession determined by using the Displacement Factor matches Newcomb's exceptionally well.

The earliest known historical records that refer to an equinoctial year always have it beginning in Taurus, never in Gemini or earlier. The civilized ability to understand the orbital and precessional astronomy was apparently imparted to known historic peoples after the beginning of the "Age of Taurus." It does seem strange that civilization sprang up rather suddenly after 4000 B.C. Something impelled mankind to begin making strides toward civilization after several thousand years of living an existence that has left no trace for our modern archeologists to dig up. Atlantis sunk about 9,000 years before Plato's time. Why did people not build cities and lasting stone monuments between that time and 4000 B.C.?

History shows that the Egyptians of the Old Kingdom built stone structures every bit as lasting as the later Egyptians. More than a thousand years of civilization didn't appreciably sharpen their abilities to build. The theory has been advanced that as man learns more things, new innovations come more rapidly. Thus 10 years of today's technology will produce much more innovation than 1,000 years of ancient Egyptian technology—except that this formula doesn't hold up for the times of the beginning of civilization. Something must have come along to rattle the slumbers of the people shortly before 4000 B.C. Could that "something" have been the mysterious Hyksos, who *taught* by example?

The Age of Taurus ushered in civilization. Written language itself helps prove this thesis. The earliest form of the Semitic language alphabet began with *alap* or *aleph,* which signifies a bull. The letter A actually began as a symbol for the horns of the bull. The symbol for bull was used by people living around the Mediterranean before the dawn of the Egyptian dynasties. Sir Flinders Petrie showed that the letter was used prior to the time of Mena in Egypt. The peoples of the earliest civilizations all worshipped the bull. Why? Was it because the bull was so strong and fine an animal they thought it was a god? Of course not; there is nothing suggestive of deity in a cud-chewing, tail-swatting bull. Apis was worshipped because of the Zodiacal sign that was information handed down to the early peoples by the civilized remnant.

In any case, the Great Pyramid marks the dawning of the Age of Taurus, and it has survived the passage of the Ages of Aries and Pisces. Now, in its unique and amazing way, it clearly marks the dawning of the newest age. The problems of the "cusp" between Aquarius and Pisces is solved by using the ancient 60-degree sign of the "Fish Man." The borders are clear-cut for the earlier sign. So if we were to stand on the Great Pyramid's truncated top at midnight, August 20, 1953, and project our meridian out into the night sky, we would intersect a point exactly halfway between the original signs' borders. The plane of the axis is wobbling out of the Pisces side and into the Aquarius side.

There is an interesting sidelight to this stargazing from the top of the Great Pyramid. Were we to stand there at midnight of the autumnal equinox in the year 4000 B.C., or, more precisely, as we began the equinoctial year 3999 B.C.—the starting point of the Great Pyramid's chronological scale—we could project our meridian, the ecliptic, and the celestial equator out, and all three would join at a point exactly equidistant between the two stars marking the points of the horns of Taurus. Now, if you wish to compute the lunar cycles, you can prove this: at the same time a gorgeous full moon was in the exact same spot. We have all seen the ancient Egyptian sculpture depicting the god or king wearing a hat with a round ball-like thing between two horns. Until now, we've had no rationale for such a headdress design.

At lectures, I am invariably asked: "If we entered the Age of Aquarius in 1953 and started down the south wall of the chamber, is there any-

126

thing else to perhaps indicate what's coming up?" Ah, yes! The old bugaboo—predictions. Indeed there seems to be a way to get some more perpendiculars to strike the timeline—the sarcophagus for instance—but we've run out of an important ingredient, the allegory. I can toss out several dates obtained by measuring the perimeter of the King's Chamber—the Chamber of Judgment—but there is no way to assign significance or meaning. We had the veil of conflict for August 5, 1914, to November 11, 1918. We have no allegory for, say, February 1977.

Incidentally, that is correct—but so what? If it is indeed significant, we'll find out. If it isn't, we'll probably be too busy to miss it. The outworking of free will dictates the future.

As for the "new age," it seems as though the 1950s indeed brought the beginnings of sweeping social changes. I can remember how so many of us eagerly awaited our discharge papers from the military following the end of the Korean "War," and immediately following the final red tape, we burned our sea bags symbolically. Veterans of the Korean War were truly the first to announce defiantly that they were "fed up with war." Of course, all veterans of all wars came away tired of killing, but the "glory" of battle was still a big psychological factor in the mass thinking. Even after World War II, our country had the "glory" glow. But with the dawning of the new age, the common soldier, sailor, and airman began to show that they were repulsed by the nonsense of fighting. It wasn't a massive movement like the later Vietnam antiwar demonstrations, but it was the beginning of a new, enlightened kind of thinking.

Despite the obvious threat of Communism, many people were saying, "There's a better way to solve problems. Unless an aggressive enemy is landing on my shores, I'll never fight again."

For 2,000 years the Christian churches preached doctrines of peace and love on Sunday, and did battle the rest of the week. Suddenly, in the mid-1950s, people—especially the young with full lives ahead of them—began to rebel against the established notions that it is honorable to go to war. The symptoms of sweeping change began to show in the late 1950s. The first "sit-down strike" by students in 1958 is one example.

Of course, not all the activity of change was for the highest good at the time it happened. When social change comes, it always brings confusion, and the confusion breeds controversy and sometimes violence. But, after all, violence had been the way to solve problems in the past; why not now? The conditioned response is as much to blame for the riots in the streets and on the campuses as are the agitators who tried to take advantage of the social unrest.

No matter how patriotic a person may feel today, regardless of how bitter they may be at the deserters and draft dodgers of the Vietnam conflict, people know in their hearts that war is the greatest insanity of man. The difference between the Aquarian Age and the Piscean Age is that a huge block of people will have the courage and fortitude to stand up against tradition and deeply rooted "glory" thinking, and refuse to fight or kill.

This is not the time or the place to argue the merits of defending oneself in case of reasonable attack. There are the pacifists who would even refuse violence in the face of such aggression. What has commenced with the new age, clearly marked in the Great Pyramid, is the essence of "new age thinking." First, we must take the initial step—rebel against war—then we can begin to find solutions to the unsolved problems built up by bitterness and hate and negativity for the past twenty centuries. We may not solve the problems immediately. However, the seeds of right thinking have been sown that will enable mankind to progress and break the war cycle.

CHAPTER NINE

The Sermon in the Pyramid

Nothing could be more solid, nor more concrete an example of man's perfection, than the Great Pyramid. What kind of people could have built such a monument? That question is so mind-boggling that many great thinkers, after seeking the answer, ultimately determined that man had to have help from Divinity to build such a perfect structure. How else could such accurate prophecy have been made? How else could ancient builders know the size of the planet would provide a unit of measure —that would coincide with the universal geometric relationship of diameter to circumference; that would intrinsically involve the number of days in the solar year; that would in turn describe the number of years in the precessional circuit?

Piazzi Smyth, John Taylor, and even David Davidson could not attribute these abilities to man alone. This is where I differ with those brilliant and courageous men who upheld the facts they discovered in the Pyramid. There is no way we can separate God from man if we accept that man was created in God's image. I accept that, and the Great Pyramid demonstrates an important aspect of that idea of creation.

You and I and everyone on this planet are the spitting image of our Creator—not as we are when we walk around bungling, bellyaching, and brutalizing, but in the makeup of our individualism. Every human being is a discreet bundle of mental energy, and every one of us has exactly the same qualities of mind—the "image" of our Creator: memory, will, desire, consciousness, conscience, creativity, curiosity, reason, emotion, and intuition. These are the same qualities inherent in the Creator, except that in humankind they are relatively undeveloped. The job of every Ego, every individual bundle of mental energy, is to "glorify" the Creator by progressing from undeveloped clods to God. We have the tools, and we are granted thousands of lifetimes to learn to use them. If you object to the idea of reincarnation, you must figure out a way to develop your qualities of mind and be the equal of your Creator in one lifetime. I suppose it could be done. I can't see that we are limited by anything except our individual efforts.

There are those who have moved considerably farther along the path to the Creator than the rest of us. These are the "elders," the Egos who know a great deal more of the truth of the universe than the rest of us—despite our education and degrees. They often walk among us and show us, by their example, how to improve ourselves. Just as the Hyksos walked among the early inhabitants of the Nile valley and showed by example.

The monument built on the plateau at Giza is a magnificent example.

One thing is tremendously important to know—people cannot *teach* others anything; others *learn*. You could go from door to door preaching your philosophy of love and brotherhood, but you would have few listeners if you did not set an example of what you preached. And if any of those listeners were to *learn* from you, it would not be from your words but from your example. The greatest Teacher of them all actually said very little—Christ's dispensation was a two and a half year example. He was such an example of what He taught that His words had a far more profound effect than those of any other individual in history.

The sermon in the Great Pyramid thunders forth in silence. Man can be perfect, and we should never settle for less. Human beings, exactly like you and me, over the course of many lifetimes and with the help of great civilizations (as ours could be, but so far is not), progressed themselves to the point of being able to erect such a structure and *know the future.*

As we grow in character, it is natural for our mental abilities to expand, and eventually we will become aware of the other levels of existence, in which time, as we know it on the physical level, has no meaning. Once an individual evolves to a point many people like to call "cosmic consciousness," that person can consciously move in time like H. G. Wells' time machine. In the future you can see the outworkings of free will—just as the builders of the Great Pyramid saw the outworkings of free will and man's ignorance bring on the great war of 1914.

The message of the Great Pyramid tells us: we have the tools to make it past the Gate of Ascent, and to work our way up the Hall of Truth in Darkness until we reach a level of awareness that leads us into the Hall of Truth in Light.

When we reach the Floor of the Temple and complete our progess for this life wave, we will look back and want to help those Egos who are struggling, or who are tumbling down toward chaos in their ignorance and pride. We will then realize that the law of the Creator states that every Ego, created in his image, *must* make the ascent, must return to perfection, on his own. We cannot lead others by the hand, regardless how much we may wish to do so. We can only be examples to them; we can only demonstrate that such perfection is possible.

Here we are, living in the twentieth century. Our technology is utterly fantastic. Our morals generally disgusting. Civilization is mankind's way of helping man grow toward perfection, but one would never think this by looking at our civilization. But it's not all bad; there is much that is good in what we've accomplished, slowly, over the past twenty centuries. We have freedom of choice and movement. We are no longer subjected to the dictates of tyrants and dogmas. We have evolved an educational system with tremendous promise— there's a great deal more to learn, but the system is evolving. The freedoms granted individuals by the United States Constitution are one of the key steps in the Great Plan to evolve civilization from the calamity of Pharaoh to the Nation of God.

The United States, for all its present-day faults, has done its job. Perhaps that is why the thoughtful forefathers had the image of the Great Pyramid engraved on our national seal.

The new age is here. There is a growing restlessness in more and more people as their intuition tells them that we are on the verge of even more profound change. I recall walking in the Chicago Loop one foggy Sunday morning. The tremendous activity that was omnipresent during the rest of the week was down to a trickle. Here and there in the dim, misty light a lonely figure scurried from one point to another. I was walking beneath the elevated train tracks when I heard the sound of an alarm. The few other people on the street also heard the alarm. A store was being broken into somewhere nearby. At first impulse I wanted to investigate, but my second nature, honed by city living, dictated that I not interfere. What could I possibly do? I asked myself. The others glanced furtively in the direction of the alarm and hastened away, not wanting to become involved. The alarm continued sounding as I walked away. Slowly the sound faded out of my hearing, but I knew the alarm was still vibrating into the cool morning air.

The events of our world today are a lot like that morning in Chicago's Loop. There is an alarm sounding, and all of us can hear it. Most of us don't want to be involved. What can we possibly do? we ask ourselves.

We have two choices. We can heed the warning and react, or we can scurry out of earshot. The vast majority will do the latter. They will try to avoid involvement and get caught up in the juggernaut of violence the future appears to be bringing. The outworkings of free will and ignorance have created insurmountable problems. Though violence will not provide a solution, history indicates our world will react violently.

What can we do if we heed the warning, because we will surely be in the minority? We can work on ourselves and build strength of character so that we can be an example. Like the Phoenix, those who strive will arise from the ashes and lead the way to better things.

According to many sources, our world is headed for economic collapse, atomic war, and finally another cataclysm. These are terrible prospects. But such events have occurred before. Greater civilizations than ours have risen and sunk. The job, then, for those who heed the alarm and prepare, is to salvage the greatness of our civilization and preserve it for the new civilization ahead.

A big noise is being made these days about our "heritage." All mankind has the same heritage. A magnificent, concrete example of that heritage was left in the land of Egypt. The Great Pyramid is truly Man's Monument to Man.

APPENDIX I

The Scientific Mystique

The Great Pyramid's purpose is one of aiding mankind by caling attention to human perfection; thus it stands to reason that anything scientific can be intrinsic to the strucure. The scientific mystique emanating from the monuments at Giza continues to attract eminent scholars as much today as it did a century ago. Brilliant men of science, who scoff at any theory other than the tombic theory, have gone to great technological and scientific lengths to probe further into the huge structures in search of additional chambers and buried treasure.

Reasoning that the system of passages and chambers within the Great Pyramid is more elaborate and complete than in the second pyramid, some scientists feel it is useless to attempt to find a secret chamber with the mummified remains of Khufu or Cheops, so they aimed sophisticated equipment in the direction of the Great Pyramid's second-rate imitator, hoping to find amid the bulk of that structure the equally lost remains of Chephren—and of course the jewels and gold that must also be there.

The second pyramid has a far simpler interior design than the Great Pyramid. The entrance is on the north side, and slightly descending passages lead to a chamber or vault at the base, in the center of the structure. Since these men of science are not convinced that the Great Pyramid was built thousands of years before the second pyramid by an entirely different group of people for an entirely different purpose, they reason that burial chambers could well be located above the baseline vault. In 1967 *Popular Science* magazine told the story of this "scientific" endeavor. The headline read: "Atom Sleuths Seek Secret Treasures in the Pyramids." The sub-headline read: "An X-ray search will test a fascinating theory that the inner chambers found so far were decoys for thieves—and that hidden ones, perhaps filled with riches, still await discovery."

This "fascinating" theory was going to be tested to the tune of $250,000. Most of that money was paid by you and me in the form of taxes. The sponsors for the project were the U.S. Atomic Energy Commission (AEC) and the Smithsonian Institute in cooperation with the United Arab Republic.

The story in *Popular Science* refers with regularity to "pyramids;" this seems to convey a meaning that if the atom sleuths were successful in discovering and excavating burial vaults in Chephren's alleged pyramid tomb, they might tackle the Great Pyramid after all. The magazine, in typical inflationary disregard for expenditures of tax dollars, also stated that "now, for the first time in history, it has become feasible to find out." Hit-or-miss tunneling through the pyramids would be prohibitively laborious and costly—but ultra-modern atomic equipment offers a way to "X-ray" a pyramid for secret chambers.

It is my considered opinion that for $250,000, one could get Arab laborers to dismantle the entire second pyramid.

That these physicists were serious indicates the hold on thinking that "expertise" has—the atom sleuths were proceeding on a tombic theory that is shaky, to say the least, especially with regard to the Great Pyramid. Dr. Luis Alvarez, an "atomic" scientist, proposed the idea, and Dr. Ahmed Fah-kry, UAR authority on Egyptian antiquities, was said to go along with the notion. They installed "spark chambers" as cosmic ray detectors in the 46 by 16 by 20-foot chamber in the center-base of the second pyramid, with a computer reading the results intended to get an X-ray picture of the pyramid's interior—revealing the secret tomb rooms.

By 1968 the project cost had gone to $500,000, and the physicists were anticipating international fame. Something didn't work, though. The project was bungled and the experts disagreed on why. It seemed as though they had learned their lesson, but no, Stanford Research Institute got into the act and revived the program. They are still trying to X-ray the second pyramid, and if they do find any mummies lying around, they still have the mystery of the Great Pyramid on their hands. The tombs of Khufu and Chephren were prepared long after the Great Pyramid was erected.

One of the problems encountered by the physicists, whose idea wasn't really so bad, despite my obvious prejudice, was that the sophisticated equipment did not work as predicted. Something caused it to go amiss. Dr. Alvarez reported to the American Physical Society in 1974 that there have been many "tantalizing" findings. It appeared originally they had struck paydirt, but all turned out to be false hopes. Alvarez has never admitted that the so-called "pyramid effect" had anything to do with the failure of his equipment to do the job it was designed to do.

The "pyramid effect" is the most celebrated of the recent scientific curiosities to emerge from the faddish study of the Great Pyramid. It is demonstrated regularly that the unusual shape of the Great Pyramid causes unexplained effects on certain physical materials—especially organic matter. Precisely what takes place is a mystery to science, which has just begun to take serious notice of the phenomenon. However, like every other scientific aspect of the Great Pyramid, this unusual "effect" generated controversy. Most advocates of the theory that the shape generates some as yet unknown form of energy by its geometric perfection believe the energy interfered with the cosmic ray machinery.

The popular book *Psychic Discoveries Behind the Iron Curtain*, by Shelia Ostrander and Lynn Schroeder, is generally credited with starting the hullabaloo over the "pyramid energy." However, this book was published in 1970 and related a relatively recent story of the "discovery" of the unexplained energy by a Frenchman named Bovis. Back in 1929 at the University of Cincinnati a professor of physics named Samuel James McIntosh Allen told his students about the unusual properties of the geometric pyramid shape.

In 1935, John Hall of Chicago experimented with a model pyramid and duplicated many of the experiments being ballyhooed today. In addition, Mr. Hall told me he demonstrated that some sort of electric charge came off the apex by using a copper ring and two very long leads of copper wire. The notion of the "pyramid effect" isn't as new as today's faddists would have us believe, but it is certainly publicized as never before—and science is now taking a serious look at this latest aspect of the Great Pyramid's scientific mystique.

Ostrander and Schroeder told how Bovis, while visting inside the Great Pyramid, discovered the bodies of animals that had died within the structure and were tossed into waste receptacles did not putrefy as would be expected of decaying bodies. He tested one of the bodies and found it totally dehydrated, but without the usual accompanying rot. In effect, the rodent cadavers were mummified. He was further baffled by the condition when he noted that the humidity index was high. Bovis returned to Paris and made a wooden model of the pyramid and tossed a dead cat inside. The same thing hapened. Despite the humid Paris air, the cat's body inside the pyramid shape dehydrated without putrefaction. The report Bovis wrote on his findings came to the attention of Karl Drbal, a noted Czech radio engineer, who carried the research a step further.

Drbal had been a soldier in his youth, and while marveling at the apparent "pyramid effect" on biological matter, he recalled that moonlight had a strange effect on carbon steel blades of straight razors—many times pranksters in the army would open another soldier's blade to moonlight and dull it. Drbal tested the pyramid effect on ordinary carbon steel or "blue" blades and discovered it worked the opposite of moonlight—a blade dulled by use seemed to return to its original sharpness after spending some time within a pyramid model.

Drbal applied for a novelty patent and obtained it for his "Cheops Pyramid Razorblade Sharpener." After the Ostrander-Schroeder book was published, the razorblade sharpening and dehydration effect models popped up everywhere. Max Toth of New York acquired Drbal's patent rights, and every Tom, Dick, and Harry in the country—including myself—either made a model or bought one after hearing about it. I obtained the precision built plexiglass models built by the late John Dilley of Chicago. The Dilley models are sold by Edmunds Scientific and have been featured in a number of school science fairs.

Dilley and I both tried the razor blade experiments of shaving with the blade until it bit our faces, then placing it inside a model, aligning the blade and the model north-south and shaving again in twenty-four hours. Dilley obtained eighty-four shaves with one ordinary blue blade, and probably could have gone on longer with it.

Of course these are highly subjective experiments and are more fun than they are scientific—but something definitely takes place. I arranged to send Dilley models to several scientists at various institutions, but have not received reports yet. I was unable to get any comment from the Gillette company about the effect, despite three letters to their research and development people.

Although I have treated it lightly, the subject of the pyramid effect is a serious matter, and perhaps as our best scientific minds seriously investigate, they will unlock a vast new principle. Somehow, after studying the Great Pyramid for so many years, I feel the wise old builders planned it this way so that we could benefit scientifically as well as philosophically.

One of my own experiments is of particular significance. I used six small pudding bowls and painstakingly floated sewing needles on top of about two inches of water. The floating needles pointed in random directions, and I was careful not to try this where electronic gear or magnetic influences could interfere. I placed a Dilley model over each bowl and within a few minutes the needle, each time, pointed to magnetic north like a compass. There's a catch, however. I was absolutely certain in my mind that the needles would become magnetized by the pyramid effect, and they apparently did. A friend, not at all sure this would happen, tried the very same experiment, and it failed. The first thing that comes to my mind is that human thought may have a profound effect when directed to interrelate with the pyramid effect. I'm convinced that thoughts are able to generate energy fields, and apparently so can the shape of the Great Pyramid.

The dehydration without rotting process is easily the most fascinating for amateur experimenters. After all, one can see the results clearly and share them with others objectively. A French experimenter, Jean Marital, used ungutted small fish for several dehydration experiments. He weighed the fish carefully, then placed it inside a model pyramid. After several days, the fish showed no signs of decay and decomposition; rather they dehydrated and preserved most of the original coloring and markings. Marital noted that the overall average amount of dehydration in all his experiments was 66 percent of the body weight.

The idea that the pyramid shape can preserve foods is an old one, especially in Europe. And the notion that certain geometric shapes cause unusual, exciting things goes back to Pythagoras —who studied in Egypt, so it probably goes back even farther. Perhaps it goes back to Atlantis or Lemuria.

One thing is certain about the pyramid effect. It has captured the fancy of many people today, both dabblers and serious students. One of the most ardent investigators of the pyramid effect is Pat Flanagan of Glendale, California. Flanagan authored a book on the subject, *Pyramid Power,* which was published by DeVorss. Flanagan is acknowledged as a genius by many scientists who have worked with him. He's certainly eccentric, but then many men of genius are. Flanagan studied, measured, and metered the various "energy fields" involved with the pyramid shape and developed some extremely interesting products. He patented a magnetic cylinder device that duplicates the energy fields within the pyramid and can be used to "purify" water. This water purifier is still in the development stage, but initial tests indicate that brackish water can be made potable by running it through the cylinder. Bacteria are killed by the energy fields; this could account for the dehydration without putrefaction process within the pyramid. Particles of solids in the water are literally "exploded" and suspended colloidally by the force fields.

While this new field of technology is in its infancy, we have had some enjoyable moments with it. The Flanagan cylinder will take the menthol out of cigarettes to a remarkable degree by simply dropping the cigarette down the pipe-sized hole in the middle of the cylinder. It is fun to dementholate someone's Kools and watch his expression when he lights up. One excited friend discovered a marketable use for the device even if it fails to purify water adequately—he learned that by pouring his ordinary bar Scotch through the cylinder, he had a drink as smooth as Chivas Regal.

Flanagan developed a device he calls the "pyramid generator." This device seems to improve the flavor of certain foods and drinks by merely placing the food or drink container on top of the device.

Flanagan, using the techniques of high-voltage photography, called Kirlian photography after the Russian inventor, actually photographed the energy emanating from the pyramid generator's apex points. The exterior energy of the pyramid effect is as profound as the interior effect. Flanagan's generators cover a small table in his home. He heaps fruit in a wooden bowl atop the generators, and the fruit stays fresh for a surprising length of time. Flanagan points out that it may be possible to ship fresh fruits and vegetables over long distances without expensive refrigeration by merely putting the layers of the product between rows of pyramid generators.

What makes the pyramid effect work? Flanagan is convinced that the pyramid energy changes the "di-electric" properties of matter. He contends that the di-electric energy is a reflection of the electrical charge on the surface of a body of matter. His detailed findings have not been published yet, but essentially this is what he has discovered:

He refers to Michael Faraday's classical experiment with the cone-shaped silk bag to demonstrate the distribution of electrical charge over an isolated body. "He charged the silk bag with static electricity and found all the charge was concentrated around the exterior of the cone, but no charge was inside. He pulled a string and reversed the bag inside-out; the charge was transferred to the outside with no charge remaining inside. The conclusion is that all static charge lies on the surface of a body."

Flanagan then realized that the distribution of surface charges on a pyramid would provide a concentration of force at the apex. These basics were augmented by a recent technological breakthrough in which an electrical field accompanied by ion emission is capable of instantly cooling white-hot steel by thousands of degrees. As it remains with most electric technology, no thorough explanation of this action has been worked out. Flanagan developed a device he calls his electronic differential thermometer. He can detect minute temperature differentials between two probes. Using this and other meters he developed, Flanagan claims he has discovered an approximation of the exact nature of the unusual energy.

Flanagan said, "The energy content in a pyramid varies according to the time of day, season, weather, phases of the moon and the polarity and quantity of ions in the surrounding atmosphere. The failures and successes of pyramid model experiments depend on a complex arrangement of environmental factors, and to some extent they can be affected by the mind." I was pleased with the latter part of his conclusion, as it matched my own. Of course, that proves nothing.

Flanagan continued: "The most important factors isolated for pyramid effects are the alignment of the pyramid to *magnetic* north and the quantity and polarity of atmospheric electricity in the form of free ions." Flanagan has since developed a negative ion generator that does not emit dangerous ozone. It is generally accepted that negatively charged particles in the atmosphere are beneficial to human behavior and a sense of well-being. Flanagan claims it actually has a beneficial physical effect.

Flanagan detected an increase of energy in and above the pyramid shape by an increase in the negative ion content in the atmosphere. He related the temperature change to the technological temperature change in cooling metals with electricity. Flanagan believes the natural ion plasma surrounding a pyramid shape is the single most important factor of its energy, while the focusing effect of magnetic fields is of secondary importance

Flanagan seeks to enlarge the physics of the electric charge. He points out that it is universal to balance all accounts, so there can be positive and negative, neutral and zero.

The thing to remember is that if Flanagan's work proves out, we owe it all to the mystique of the Great Pyramid of Giza. Flanagan went on: "The earth itself is a huge sphere negatively charged in respect to the ionosphere of 400,000 volts. The surface of the earth is negative, the center of the earth is *zero* charge. The interior is somehow extremely hot, by thousands of degrees. Where does the temperature come from? The earth is hot for the same reason that a pyramid is hotter inside than outside . . . because of the differential between charge and zero charge. This flow of energy could be related to gravitation and other unexplained phenomena."

Flanagan feels the pyramid shape creates an electric vacuum inside, but not necessarily an energy field vacuum. He explained. "Dr. Otto Brunler, who researched life energy fields, called life energy 'di-electric biocosmic energy.'" His name for it is correct in my opinion. Di-electric energy is the result of the Faraday effect in the pyramid. This could explain the temperature effects in the human body to some extent. Di-electric energy is a reflection of electric charge on the surface of a body.

The detection of voltages on the surface of the body was a subject of more than 30 years' research by Dr. Harold Burr of Yale University, [Flanagan continued.] His book, *The Fields of Life*, covers some of his discoveries. For example, he was able to detect illness before it occurred, cancer, ovulation and so forth by measuring voltage fields on the surface of the skin. The measure of voltages coincident with the acupuncture points on the surface of the body is a direct reflection of the di-electric energy functions on the interior of the body. This explains, for the first time, some of the discoveries of the effects of ions, magnetic fields, light, color and other energies on the human body.

Flanagan is further convinced that the cavities in the brain and interior of the body are "accumulators of di-electric energy." He said:

> The electric counterparts on and above the surface of the body are reflections of the di-electric fields inside. The same is true of the interior of any hollow object with a charged atmosphere around it.
>
> I've discovered that the shape of the di-electric field determines some of its functions, which explains the effects of the pyramid with respect to other shapes. The phenomena of change of temperature with very little energy except for electrostatic charges and ions require serious investigation by modern technology.
>
> By definition, di-electric energy flows to areas of least charge and appears to exhibit negative entropy. The flow to areas of least charge explains why it has been observed to accumulate in organic insulators such as wood, plastic and silk. This is why the pyramid generators I developed have such a measurable effect on water.

Flanagan, who is scoffed at by many other physicists, feels the technology of di-electric fields and biocosmic energy fields will be greatly accelerated when he completes his work on new, more sophisticated instruments. He is working on meters to detect the "di-electric constant," and one to detect what he calls "magnetic spin resonance."

The applications of such metering devices could

be tremendous, especially in the field of diagnostic medicine and nutrition. Flanagan may be scoffed at, but so were Nikola Tesla and others who eventually showed they were merely ahead of "their time." Why should anyone be "ahead of his time?" What's really being said is that the scientific community can't keep up with them because they have become experts.

In *Pyramid Power*, Flanagan sets forth his "etheric vortex theory," which could be a major step in establishing a "new" physics that takes into account the ancient and mystical concept of "planes of existence." In my opinion, the one thing the ancient pyramid-building Hyksos had that we have only begun to investigate seriously is a working concept of these levels of existence. Further study into the Great Pyramid effect and energy fields may lead us to acceptance of this concept— and thus eventually to a philosophy of life that makes more sense than the majority of philosophies prevalent today.

Further pyramid energy studies will also vindicate the persecuted scientist, Dr. Wilhelm Reich. I'm not a Reich fan, but he was definitely on to something new and fantastic when our "experts" in authority caused his books to be burned (can you believe it—book burning in America?) and had him imprisoned because he advocated a kind of healing with his unorthodox devices. He died in prison.

Actually the fact that a static charge is generated from the exterior shape of the Great Pyramid was discovered by a British inventor, Sir William Siemens, while he was actually atop the monument in Egypt. Siemens noticed a faint crackling, prickling sensation when he raised his arms while standing on the truncated top of the Great Pyramid. Friends noticed a distinct sound when he did it. When he sipped a drink from his flask, he felt a shock. Growing curious, he moistened a newspaper and wrapped it around an empty bottle, converting it into a Leyden jar, which accumulates a static charge. The bottle became increasingly charged with electricity to the point where sparks began to shoot from the device. The story has it that Siemens' Arab guide grew frightened and somewhat enraged at this demonstration of "witchcraft," so Siemens gave him a little jolt with his newfound gadget and convinced him it was magic.

Another great pyramid energy investigator was Verne Cameron, who was generally regarded as a "master" dowser. A dowser is a person who "witches" wells and finds minerals under the ground with a twitch and a twig and other such unorthodox, but highly useful, things. Cameron called the pyramid effect "energy of form," or "waves of form," and he demonstrated that the Great Pyramid replicas opened new vistas in dowsing and radiesthesia. Bill Cox of Elsinore, California, is a Cameron protégé and now carries on the late scientist's work. There are those who would balk at calling Cameron a "scientist," but, by definition, he was more a scientist than most today. Cox publishes the *Pyramid Guide*, a monthly newsletter on the subject of dowsing and energy fields. A lot of material in the newsletter doesn't fit our standard notions of "science," but we should be learning a lesson by now.

Cameron, who was able to locate water and

minerals with amazing accuracy via his dowsing, never stopped seeking a scientific explanation for his own mysterious ability. The Great Pyramid mystique opened up a totally new range of thinking on the subject for him. Cox and Cameron co-authored *Aqua-Video*, which probes dowsing in detail.

Independently, Cameron and Flanagan carried research over from the pyramid form to the cone forms and finally to spirals, which appear to emanate the same mysterious energy. One of the better "meters" for this energy is "dowsing" rods. Any person, or almost any person, can prove this. Blindfold the participant and put a pair of wire dowsing rods in his hands, then have him sweep an area with the probes where a model pyramid rests—over the apex the rods will cross without the participant's conscious effort.

Another somewhat subdued area of physical science that can be opened wide with involved studies into the pyramid effect is what some have called "radionics." This is the science of detecting the individual frequencies of particles of matter. Dr. Robert Millikan, a Nobel Prize winning physicist, said in a speech before other physicists: "Someday we will find that each of the elements of material matter vibrates at a frequency, each different from the other."

Another prize-winning physicist, Dr. I. I. Rabi of Columbia University, wrote in 1940: "Atoms can act like little radio transmitters broadcasting on ultra short waves." In an announcement about new discoveries in atomic science on December 30, 1939, the distinguished scientist suggested: "Man himself as well as all kinds of supposedly inert matter constantly emit rays. Every atom and every molecule in nature is a continuous radio broadcasting station. Those who believe in telepathy, second sight and clairvoyance have in today's announcement the first scientific proof of the existence of invisible rays which really travel from one person to another."

The pyramid effect does indeed open the door to new frontiers of science—and it is fitting that it does so in light of its purpose. Now the problem of application must be solved. Edgar Mitchell, the astronaut and physicist turned phenomena researcher, once pointed out that we could never have put a man on the moon without resorting to the "systems" approach. Mitchell suggests that science use a systems approach to phenomena, including pyramid energy fields, thus combining all the specialties into a workable unit.

The Great Pyramid suggests many things to probing minds, and once again we see part of its purpose. One researcher, Alfred Dunning of Topanga Canyon, California, wrote the following in Bill Cox's *Pyramid Guide:*

Music from the Pyramid. I became interested in the history and construction of an obscure musical instrument at the same time a fascination for the pyramid awakened. I realized a hammer-struck stringed instrument resembling the known design of the ancient Santur must have existed within the cultural fabric of the people who designed and built the pyramids on the Giza plateau.

Using the measurements and harmonic geometric proportions encapsulated in the monumental structure of the Cheops Pyramid, I designed an instrument essentially based on a meridian cross-section of the pyramid with the height of one royal cubit and base of one megalithic yard. The angle of the base to side is 51 degrees, 51 minutes, and the small pyramid is in exact scale or proportion to the Cheops Pyramid.

The height is bisected to form a truncated pyramid of one-half royal cubit and a top of one-half megalithic yard. There are 72 strings (360 ÷ 5) arranged in 18 courses of four strings each. The movable pyramid bridges are placed at intervals of 3/5 to 2/5 and 4/5 to 1/5. For materials, I chose Indian Rosewood and vertical grain spruce with brass and steel strings.

The sound quality of the finished instrument, greatly enhanced by the harmonic internal angles of the soundbox, gives haunting and sustained echoes produced at the slightest string vibration. The volume capacities are impressive—filling a room with music. Tone qualities are richly varied with crystal, bell-like trebles and resounding bass tones.

I am currently experimenting with the infinite tuning possibilities and would be interested if any readers have ideas or theories on ancient scales or modes. The instrument has a four-octave range with intervals of natural fifths.

Dunning concluded by speculating that, "megalithic sites, such as Woodhenge, were originally used as musical instruments that brought celestial harmonies to the terrestrial realm." And so, it would appear that the scientific shape of the Great Pyramid may lead us to a way of truly and physically obtaining the "music of the spheres." And why not, isn't it a geometric replica of a sphere?

If you are interested in taking up any areas of pyramid research, you can contact Dunning and others through the *Pyramid Guide*, P.O. Box 176, Lake Elsinore, California 92330. At my lectures

I invariably find that students want to look into pyramid-effect research for a science fair project. The best start for anyone would be to read the book, *Exploring the Great Pyramid Shape in America*, by Kim Russell of Shapeous Researching in Dallas, Texas. Russell explains many of Flanagan's ideas in layman's terms and has done intensive study himself to add credibility to some of his ideas. Information can be obtained by writing to Russell at 5774 Leona St., Dallas, Texas 75231. I've met a number of self-appointed pyramid researchers, and the most thorough and understandable to date has been Russell.

An aspect of science and engineering totally unrelated to the mysterious energy has provided one of the most unusual and intriguing theories regarding the origin, purpose, and methods of construction of the Great Pyramid. The theory belongs to Edward J. Kunkle of Warren, Ohio, author of *Pharaoh's Pump*. Kunkle, like everyone else who tried to determine how the Great Pyramid could have been built by ancient peoples, toyed with several possible methods of construction, and resolved that the only method that could have moved the millions of tons of stone for construction was water or hydraulic engineering.

Many thinkers have advanced the theory that canals were dug to float the blocks close to the building site. Kunkle makes an interesting case for the use of locks and pumps to actually erect the structure. When he finished his study, Kunkle claimed the Great Pyramid's interior system of passages and chambers were in effect a huge pump, capable of spewing water at tremendous pressure—perhaps irrigating much of the arid desert countryside.

To arrive at his conclusions, Kunkle first mused about how anyone at any time might move material. He listed the possibilities as follows:

I made a list of the basic methods by which mass can be moved and found there were seven:

1. Manually.

2. The use of the wedge, or the screw, or the inclined plane.

3. The lever. The use of gear wheels, the pulley, and the crane.

4. The expansion of a gas, or the changing of the pressure of a gas, such as the internal combustion engine, the steam engine, the use of dynamite, a windmill or an airplane.

5. The buoyancy of a gas, as it is used in a dirigible.

6. The use of a magnet or magnetic fields, which includes the whole field of electricity.

7. By use of pumps, hydraulics or water power.

Those seven basics remain unchanged, Kunkle insists.

Before he tackled the problems of building the Great Pyramid with water power, Kunkle tackled the huge stone door that hung on pivots the size of bowling balls at the Temple of Karnak. The slab for the door weighed eighty tons. How did the temple builders manage to elevate that huge door and set it on the pivots? Kunkle decided they built a lock around the precise location of the door, filled the lock with water, floated the door into place slightly above the pivots and let the water out, allowing the door to sink slowly into position without effort.

The idea was so simple that it had to be correct, Kunkle reasoned. He then began to research the ruins at Karnak in earnest. He learned that while some of the temples were hewn from solid rock, the ground plans of the ones made of masonry showed that the temples themselves were surrounded by "girdle walls." According to Kunkle: "These are rough walls of earth, such as an excavator might hastily throw up with a bulldozer."

Kunkle also discovered something else about Egyptian temple building:

Within the girdle walls, which surround the temple of Mut, is found the remains of a *sacred lake*. The sacred lake is positive proof that in times long past, this enclosure had water in it.

I assumed that these enclosures formed by girdle walls, were in ancient times storage or catch-basins wherein water was impounded for use as a lifting medium in temple construction.

Some more facts about the temples:

They were never completely roofed over, but for the most part were open to the sky.

Each temple had a high tower of "keep" higher than the temple walls.

All faced the river.

And, at the Temple of Karnak is found a series of stone terraces leading away from it toward the river; and that these terraces are of regular size and shape, and form a sort of stairway, which is called "the avenue of the Sphinxes."

These terraces are 105 feet long, and there is no monolith within the temple more than 67 feet in length.

I toyed with the idea that these terraces could be the remains of a series of water-locks, which had been walled in and that the 67-foot monoliths could have been floated up the river on barges, up through the 105 foot locks and into the temple, then erected in a manner somewhat like that of the 80 ton door.

The more Kunkle attacked the problem of moving and placing huge blocks of stone, the more certain he was that locks were the answer. He reasoned that the Egyptians did most of their building when the Nile was at flood stage; therefore the water was closer to the building sites than during the rest of the year. Even with the swollen river close by, Kunkle reasoned that the builders needed more than a "bucket brigade" to provide the thousands of acre-feet of water necessary to build some of the huge temples and pyramids. That's when he started searching for a "pump."

He read in known documents how the ancient Egyptians were capable of fantastic canal-building projects. One was how Senusert III built a "fairway" around the second cataract of the Nile to help his troops chase Nubians. The "fairway," Kunkle concluded, was a system of locks and canals around the cataract, similar to the Welland Canal in Ontario, which allows shipping to circumvent Niagara Falls.

Finally, in the midst of his mental probing, Kunkle reasoned that the Egyptians were certainly capable of building and using "butterfly" valves for controlling the water flow rates. Digging carefully through the written words of Herodotus and other ancient historians, Kunkle noticed several curious references to water use and water flow. For example, there was a reference to a "queen who avenged a murder by drowning the members of a feast." Kunkle noted the original passage read: "As they dined, she turned the river upon them by a great hidden conduit."

To open such a conduit, even for gravity flow purposes, there had to be a valve mechanism. Kunkle claims that tourists visiting the Great Pyramid view the ruins of butterfly valves within the passage system and don't know what they are seeing.

Granite and limestone blocks can indeed make solid, workable watergates. Kunkle considers the granite leaf within the antechamber of the Great Pyramid to have originally been such a watergate. He is certain that a massive butterfly valve was placed in the grotto of what is now called the well shaft of the Pyramid's interior—and this valve controlled the flow of air and water, which made the Great Pyramid a massive water pump.

Sound silly? I don't think it's as silly as the accepted tombic theory—but I don't believe the Great Pyramid was designed solely as a pump.

Kunkle brilliantly proves his point by pumping water with a series of basins and pipes he made that match the corridor and chamber system of the Great Pyramid. Kunkle explains that the Great Pyramid's interior system is built in such a way as to embody the laws of hydraulic engineering. He goes to great lengths to show how the Grand Gallery, for example, is a perfect "vacuum bottle" in this pumping system. He even figures that the Sphinx was the secondary pump closer to the river and makes a case for that viewpoint as well. Engineers can have a delightful time with Kunkle's thesis by reading his booklet, available by writing to him, 295 W. Market Street, Warren, Ohio.

A condensed version of Kunkle's theory was printed in the *Rosicrucian Digest*. I reproduce it here:

. . . Although it took thirty years to erect this pyramid, only the three months when the Nile was at flood (and when no other work could be done) were spent in its erection. That in itself suggests a relationship between water and building. Significantly enough, around the base of this great pyramid there remains in the parabolic walls a hint of an ancient catch basin. (These walls made of loose earth apparently were built up one section at a time, each section forming a cone-like mound. Hence the name parabolic walls.)

In starting a pyramid, a level platform was first cut in the rock; then shafts and passages—or perhaps better, tubes and chambers—were cut in the solid limestone. Over these, granite masonry was added to form a kind of case around which the structure could be built.

Not an odd procedure at all, but acceptable engineering practice: The machinery first. In this case, I believe, a water pump. Before you dismiss the idea as impossible, imagine the pyramid already completed to a working level of 200 feet.

Water supplied by two fountains—one on the north side and one on the south—forms a shallow pool. On the north face of the structure there is a series of locks which ascend to the pool in zig-zag fashion. The water from the pool fills these locks, which extend right down to the Nile bank.

By means of these locks, stones could be transferred from the river to special "barges" and so lifted by this artificial waterway to the shallow pool at the working level. Here they could be floated to their proper positions in the wall and fitted with no great difficulty.

What has been called "the remains of an old carriage road" may still be traced on the north side. The eight-inch holes regularly spaced along the route, however, suggest more logically that the remains are not of a "carriage road" but of a "lock system," the holes indicating anchorages for the lock gates.

But the operation of the fountains of water is as yet unexplained. To understand that, it is necessary to examine the interior of the structure. Here we find two diagonal tubes, one cut into the solid limestone below ground, the other made of ponderous masonry above ground level.

At the lower end of each is a chamber. The lower one cut in the solid rock, I have called the Compression Chamber. The upper one is referred to ordinarily as the Queen's Chamber.

The diagonals are connected by a third tube which meets each of the others at its lower end. The upper end forms a kind of funnel while the lower end is like a jet. Today we should call this kind of joining a lateral connection. A crude spiral hump in the jet would cause water passing through it to twist or spin.

In the Queen's Chamber the roof is made up of blocks 5½ feet thick while the north and south walls consist of wedge-shaped blocks with the thick side of the wedge to the inside. Pressure inside the chamber would thus cause the wall wedges to tighten.

The upper diagonal, which Egyptologists have named the Grand Gallery, also exhibits noteworthy peculiarities. It is 156 feet long, less than 7 feet wide at the bottom, and tapering to a width of some 2 feet at the top. Its ceiling is 28 feet high. The blocks forming the gallery walls are not laid in a horizontal plane but are pitched inward 5 degrees.

Such a long sloping passage seems designed to withstand outside atmospheric pressure. A fire burning in an airtight chamber at its top would form a partial vacuum, reducing atmospheric pressure and causing water to rise in the connecting tube.

Originally, this diagonal could have been sealed off from the King's Chamber by means of a granite

161

shut-off mechanism in what is known as the Antechamber. Here may still be seen grooves and slots, also semicircular cuttings above—possibly bearings for a round shaft to raise and lower slabs in the grooves or guides. One slab remains *in situ* today. It could be what is left of the original counterweight. It is my guess that originally this mechanism was operated automatically by a float.

Near the upper end of the lower diagonal is what undoubtedly was a check valve. A door must have swung inward to close on a granite seat. The door is gone, but two holes above the seat are such as could have held a round shaft to support the hinged door. Similar holes in the tube leading to the Queen's Chamber suggest a like arrangement there.

At the ground level in the connecting tube there is a cavity as large as a small bedroom. If a buoyant valve hinged at one end with a hole in its center had been placed here, it would remain open as long as the water was at rest. When the water moved downward, however, it would slam shut, creating a water hammer to prevent most of the water from escaping. Its action would be similar to a waste valve in the common water ram.

It seems evident to me that the pyramid builders were demonstrating a physical law: Water at rest in a vessel exerts a pressure on the bottom of the vessel equal to its height, regardless of the shape of the vessel. Should water in a diagonal tube move, however, it becomes a moving mass and its work must be computed by mass and velocity. Accordingly, the lower diagonal tube would have a capacity of about 80 tons while that of the upper one would be 300.

Fire creates a vacuum which causes water to rise. When the vacuum is released, water flows down through the connecting tube and through the lateral jet connection. This causes the water in the lower diagonal to move against the compressed air in the rock-hewn Compression Chamber. When the flow stops, the compressed air forces the water back up the jet to the higher level. Repeated action builds a sufficient level in the upper diagonal to allow water to be discharged at the top.

In the pyramid operation, the Queen's Chamber is the primary Compression for the upper diagonal, the King's Chamber a secondary one. It is in the King's Chamber that the discharge tubes are found.

Air is soluble in water. Its rate of solubility is increased by air pressure upon its surface, and still further increased by turbulence of water. It follows then, that if the air in the Compression Chamber is not constantly replaced, the pump would soon cease to function.

A simple experiment will prove a telling demonstration of what might be expected of a practical application: Fill a lavatory bowl with water; remove the plug and as the whirling water starts down the drain hold a lighted match near the center of it. The flame will be carried downward with the air being drawn into the drain. The average drainpipe is about one inch in diameter. In a "drain pipe" 5 feet in diameter and a "lavatory bowl" almost 20 feet across, the amount of air would be increased phenomenally.

This whirlpool, it should be remembered, is induced by the spiral hump in the lateral jet at the bottom and the funnel at the top. The floating valve gate would stay closed although the hole in it would allow air to pass through. Thus, combustion gases would be removed and the fire at the same time be supplied with flesh air.

Another very remarkable feature of the lower Compression Chamber is that in the floor is a saucer-shaped cutting with a pit in the center. The opening is in the northeast corner. Water entering this orifice would set up a rotary motion in the saucer, creating a whirlpool with its vortex in the pit.

Such action would reduce the water pressure at the corner opening, making it possible for water from the diagonal to continue to flow into the chamber at the same time increasing its velocity. The force of gravity pumps the water, and it is augmented by the water spinning in the airtight chamber.

It was one of the famous Bernoulli family who discovered that if an orifice of clean, sharp edges be attached to a tube no longer than three times its diameter, the discharge from such a tube will be increased by more than twenty-five per cent. This has become known as the principle of the standard short tube.

The clean, sharp edges are much in evidence, and the horizontal connection which joins the lower Compression Chamber to the lower diagonal *is just such a tube,* although it is 9 times longer. It must be remembered that the ancients were working with the hundred-foot head of water and a mass of 80 tons plus.

It is on the basis of such facts that I contend that the interior passages and chambers of the Great Pyramid of Gizeh were designed to be a water pump to provide water for the pools and locks whereby the immense blocks of stone could be floated into position and fixed. . . .

The science of hydraulics taken from the Great Pyramid led to a patented hydraulic ram pump, which Kunkle obtained in 1955.

Indeed, I am also convinced that locks and canals and pumps of some kind were used to build the Great Pyramid. In fact, the use of water in the construction was carried over into a number of legends about the deep tunnel beneath the Sphinx and the Great Pyramid that leads to the Nile.

However, the builders made absolutely certain there would be no confusion between the "well shaft" and the designed interior system. The well shaft was carved out of the limestone blocks after they were put in place. It is assumed by Davidson that this was done to provide a means of access to the upper chambers after the granite plugs were built into the ascending passage.

However, the Great Pyramid surely embodies the principles of hydraulics as it embodies many other scientific principles. Kunkle's notions on the use of water for placing the huge granite blocks make good sense to a number of pyramid scholars.

There are probably many other amazing and scientific aspects to the Great Pyramid that we are overlooking. They may be discovered. Regardless, the Great Pyramid has had a profound effect on our twentieth-century world—as the builders obviously intended. It is constantly in the news media in one form or another; our attention is constantly being drawn to this magnificent monument.

A few years ago some atomic scientists at Oak Ridge, Tennessee, whose main concern is atomic waste, pointed out that the Great Pyramid could safely house all the nuclear waste generated by the United States in 5,000 years. That item appeared in all the newspapers.

In 1972, a brief United States Press bulletin was printed in the Chicago *Tribune*. It read:

Cairo, Egypt (UPI)—An Egyptian archeologist has traced a secret chamber inside the great pyramid of Giza and believes it may contain the hidden mummified body of King Cheops, the newspaper *Al Gomhouria* said Wednesday.

The secret chamber lies about 60 feet below King Cheops' burial chamber, which was found empty when the pyramid was first opened, the newspaper said.

The short piece appeared September 27, 1972.

Not another word on such a discovery has come out, so it can be chalked up to one of those unsubstantiated stories sometimes bought by newsmen.

Before that, in the 1960s some tourist-bureau people announced that they wanted to build an elevator of sorts on the Great Pyramid's exterior to carry visitors to the top. The newspaper *Al Ahram* called the plan an "outrage against our ancient civilization. We shall not allow ourselves to become the laughing stock of history." And the plan was finally dropped. It's a tough climb to the top of the Great Pyramid, but many people make it. The Duke of Windsor once climbed it, then drove a golf ball off the top.

After studying the huge monument carefully, one might think that such a "fun" thing is irreverent. However, there is an old saying that "time mocks all things; the pyramids mock at time." Ironically, that's a saying from ancient Egypt. They knew what they were talking about.

APPENDIX II

Pyramid Games People Play

Many people have been suddenly swept up in a Great Pyramid "Fantasia" in recent years because the huge monument is so dramatically wonderful. With the advent of "pyramid power," the metaphysical attraction of the structure has been hyped up, sometimes beyond the limit of good sense. This final section will look into some of the games people are playing with the Great Pyramid's science and mystery. In some cases there is sure to be credence buried beneath the froth and excitement, while in others the notion is less than half-cocked.

Sometimes very serious-sounding individuals can make statements that ring so untrue that it is easy to understand why so many thinking people, upon hearing such statements, decide that the Great Pyramid must be nothing more than a tomb and that the Egyptologists are correct in considering the pyramidologists a bunch of kooks.

A dozen years ago I read an article about the last surviving member of the excavation team at King Tut's tomb—Dr. J. O. Kinnaman. The article immediately established credibility by pointing out that Dr. Kinnaman, a Biblical archeologist of excellent repute, was *not* a victim of the exploited "King Tut curse."

Kinnaman had been at the Great Pyramid when Petrie was making his famous measurements, and according to the article, he and Petrie agreed that the monument was not built by Khufu, but by "Atlanteans," some 46,000 years ago. The interviewer asked Dr. Kinnaman, "But how did you and Dr. Petrie discover all this?"

The reply was as follows:

"By accident," he said. "We discovered a secret room containing things you'd never believe, and in that secret room among other items we found proof of the date of the building of the Pyramid. We found manuscripts that told us for what purpose it was built, and we found a lot more, too."

"But how is it that we have never heard of this room?"

"Because Dr. Petrie and I swore an oath to highest government officials in Egypt and Great Britain never to divulge this knowledge during our lifetimes."

"Why not?"

"Well, it was the consensus at that time that the world in general was not yet ready to understand and cope with this knowledge, much less really believe that it actually exists!"

The reporter seemed to be digging for facts, but wound up writing that Dr. Kinnaman told much more, but it was all true. How did the reporter know? "Because it was impossible to know Dr. Kinnaman for very long without being convinced that he would never lie, rationalize, imagine, or even theorize about what might or might not be so."

It is utterly unbelievable that Sir Flinders Petrie, who set out to investigate the thesis of Piazzi Smyth, would have kept quiet about any "hidden chambers" with all that "proof" in it.

It sounds like nonsense to me that "manuscripts" telling the Pyramid's "purpose" would be written at all, since the pyramid tells its own purpose so clearly without the problems of language.

And whenever I hear anyone say that the information was withheld because the world isn't ready to "understand," I rebel.

There may be another little chamber hidden in the bulk of the Great Pyramid, and it could be filled with all kinds of fantastic scrolls—I don't pretend to know it all. But I'll bet my all that no such room is ever found, and that Dr. Kinnaman was somehow sincerely deluded about what he and Petrie discovered.

The problem, if indeed any problem exists, is that many people will believe such a thing.

Many people are convinced that a secret chamber or corridor is going to be found between the Sphinx and the Great Pyramid. I used to believe this myself. Now, I doubt if one ever existed. It isn't necessary for such a link-up to be made. One of the main reasons for this belief is that the famed medium Edgar Cayce predicted that such a hidden chamber would be found. Many other "mystical" persons and groups are also predicting the discovery of such a chamber.

A few years ago I met a psychic in Chicago who told me that he had been inside the Sphinx and had crawled along a narrow corridor toward the Great Pyramid. He had done this thing in 1945, as World War II was drawing to a close. The man told me that he had been with the attaché staff in Cairo, and one night at a party he and King Farouk got to talking "Masonic stuff," so Farouk commandeered a jeep, and the two of them rode to the Sphinx in the dead of night. The King and the Colonel approached the ancient monuments, and as the American watched in open-mouthed wonder, Farouk touched something and shoved a huge slab door open. They stepped inside the total darkness, and the American followed the King down into a narrow passage.

I confess I cannot recall the details of the remainder of the story, which went on to relate something about a large chamber and a huge guard with a sword and so forth. My mind had already started to whirl in challenge of what I was hearing, but not believing.

Later I decided that the story couldn't have been totally imagination, knowing the story-teller, so maybe there was some basis in fact. After all, hundreds of people believe such a secret corridor exists. Some friends and I actually plotted when would be the best time to visit Egypt and locate that secret passage.

If someone finds such a thing, I'll be as excited as anyone. I don't say it doesn't exist, I just doubt it.

Next to secret passages and chambers and

proofs of purpose that we would never understand, the second biggest game is the use of the pyramid effect to enhance "psychic ability."

There must be a hundred sensitives around the world who have built model pyramids to sit inside, and almost all of them are announcing how greatly improved their psychic minds become because of the mysterious energy.

I suppose that if one truly believes that meditating inside a model pyramid will enhance his "cosmic consciousness," it may be beneficial to him. After all, we are what we think. But I have yet to see any dramatic demonstration that sitting, eating, sleeping, meditating, contemplating, or making love inside a model pyramid does anything wondrous.

I have heard and read about a number of healings that have taken place inside model pyramids. None have been confirmed to my satisfaction.

One California contracting company came up with a great idea, and it should have sold well—but it didn't. They drew up plans for secondary homes made to scale of the Great Pyramid. Anyone wanting to live in the "beneficial" atmosphere of the pyramid shape could purchase these plans and turn them over to a builder, or build the home himself. Some of the designs were attractive, too.

I number among my friends one of the world's leading authorities on "cataclysmology," Chan Thomas of Los Angeles. Chan lectures on his theory and wrote a small book titled *The Adam and Eve Story*, which outlines his ideas on the cataclysms of the past and one coming up.

I feel that he has a great deal of scientific evidence for the theory he expounds, but I think that one of his facts about the Great Pyramid is misinformation. It's one of the first things I checked when I visited the Great Pyramid shortly after this writing. Chan had been told that a water mark exists all the way around the masonry of the Great Pyramid about 200 feet up from the base. I've never read any mention of such a thing, and it seems to me that Smyth, Petrie, or Davidson would have noticed it if it existed. The fundamentalists especially would have jumped on such a water mark as "proof" that the flood came after "Enoch" built the pyramid.

As far as I could tell, no such watermark was there. If such a mark exists, it woud be great evidence for the water lock system of construction.

Another game played by those with an esoteric bent is the ancient "abracadabra" pyramid bit. I've never been able to determine exactly why the pyramiding of this word should have any significance, but there are many who do attribute significance to it, and somehow link it to the Great Pyramid's mystique. Again, the Great Pyramid doesn't need any hocus-pocus to impress.

The notion that the Great Pyramid is sitting atop an ancient volcano and is actually a cover over an entrance to the "hollow earth" or the "lost Atlantis" is about as silly as any notion can get. (I'm sure to get irate letters for saying some of these things.)

One of the bigger games was played by the followers of Piazzi Smyth. Even Davidson got caught up a little with this one. This is using the "boss" or the carved bas-relief located on the granite leaf in the antechamber as a "proof" for the pyramid inch. I used such a statement in my lectures until I read Petrie more closely. Pyramidologists will say the "boss" juts out from the smooth granite block precisely one polar-diameter inch, thus monumentalizing the unit of measure. If this were clearly true, the controversy might not have been so bitter. But Petrie points out that the "boss" is about 25 square inches in area and sticks out anywhere from .94 inch to 1.07 inches. This is close to the pd-inch, but certainly, as Petrie pointed out, "Nothing more unscientific as a standard for a unit of measure can be imagined."

Another common game is for individuals who spend money on "past life readings" to be told by the medium or whatever that they were "associated" with the Great Pyramid's construction. If as many workers did the actual building as most people believe, such a statement could be true.

There are a number of amazing, odd fact games that can be played with the Great Pyramid's dimensions. For example, to determine the area of a sphere, multiply the square of the diameter by pi, which is clearly outlined in the Great Pyramid's geometry. Using the dimensions of the Great Pyramid, you will get a figure of 196,936,058 square miles for the area of the surface of the earth. The Encyclopedia Britannica lists the area figure as 196,940,000 square miles, which is a roughly rounded off figure.

The estimated total weight of the stones in the Great Pyramid is 5,273,000 tons. Some experts claim that if you add 15 zeros to that figure, you'll have the estimated weight of the earth.

The height of the Great Pyramid is said to provide a figure for the average distance between the earth and the sun. Since the elevation rises on a ratio of 10 to 9, for every 10 feet of height the pyramid slopes inward 9 feet, the game-players contend you multiply the height of 5,813 pd-inches by 10 to the ninth power. Sure enough, you'll get a figure of 91,837,484 *miles*. The generally accepted mean distance to the sun is 92 million miles, so again the numbers are close.

The temperature within the King's Chamber is said to remain a constant 68 degrees Fahrenheit. This is figured to be the average temperature of the earth's surface. This is also one-fifth the distance mercury rises between freezing and boiling at sea level; and there are those who stress that the Great Pyramid has a tremendous affinity for the number 5.

Worth Smith, who wrote and lectured on the Great Pyramid's relation to the Bible, commented on the mysterious science of numbers within the structure:

Mystic five is accented thus:

1. The Queen's Chamber floor plane is situated on the level of the 25th (5 X 5) tier of masonry.

2. All measures in this recess, so often termed the "Jew's Chamber" answer to a single standard, that of the Ancient Sacred Hebrew Cubit of 25 inches.

3. The niche in the east wall of the room is 15 feet (3 X 5) high.

4. The niche is composed of five strongly marked stories, the top story of which is 25 inches in width; the center of this top story is removed from the perpendicular center of the wall by 25 inches.

5. The King's Chamber floor plan is situated on the 50th (2 X 5 X 5) course of masonry.

6. The 35th course of masonry (5 X 7) stands out due to unusual height of the tier.

7. The walls of the King's Chamber contain 100 (4 X 5 X 5) stones.

8. Each of the four sides of the King's Chamber has 25 blocks of stone arranged in 5 tiers of 5 blocks each.

9. There are five construction chambers directly above the King's Chamber.

10. In the King's Chamber the base-line of the lowest course of stones in each of the four walls is precisely 5 inches below the floor level.

11. Deducting the 5 inches that each wall is set into the floor level, the area of the first tier of stones in each wall is precisely 50 (2 X 5 X 5) times the cubic contents of the sarcophagus. . . ."

And he can go on with other number games; for example, the mystical number seven is also found throughout the Great Pyramid:

"The length of the base is exactly seven times the length of the Grand Gallery. The Grand Gallery is exactly seven times as high as the ascending passage leading to it; there are seven overlapping tiers of stones in each of the east and west walls of the Grand Gallery.

"The altitude of the pyramid is 7/11 of the length of each side; the pyramid makes a direct and grand reference to the constellation of Pleiades, a group consisting of seven stars."

As you can see, it gets a bit far-fetched at times. Worth Smith was certain that the Great Pyramid was the "Bible in stone," and he wrote his thesis in glowing terms. He was a strong "Anglo-Israelist."

Finally, there is a belief of several "mystery schools," such as the Rosicrucians and the Theosophical Society, who are taught that the Great Pyramid was used as a place of "initiation" into the mysteries, or for individuals advancing up the ladder of Egoic evolution. I can't dispute this belief on any basis. Surely no other structure on earth would be better suited for such a purpose. It's entirely feasible that persons who understood the interior system of corridors and chambers would have entered through the cleverly concealed doorway, which swiveled like a "butterfly valve," and once inside they could have descended to the well shaft, and then made their way up into the primary chambers.

The Great Pyramid is not one thing, it is many things. It is no accident that today our society is becoming more conscious of the huge edifice that so far has defied complete translation, but has so perfectly made its point. Life itself is like that; we don't fully understand as we evolve, but the laws of the universe clearly make their point.

There's an old saying in America. You can take it or leave. That's exactly how each of us, with our free will, can react toward Man's Monument to Man.

The fascinating story behind
the greatest naval adventures of all time.
the saga of Horatio Hornblower

The Hornblower Companion

C. S. FORESTER

The complete and indispensable guide.
Fully illustrated with maps, charts, and drawings
by Samuel H. Bryant

425 44004195

DO YOU KNOW HOW TO . . . ?

(Pinnacle Books can help you)

DO YOU KNOW HOW TO?
(Pinnacle does and can help you!)

Pinnacle Books proudly presents a list of
books that can bring you new health
and increased happiness.

Check which books you'd like to own:

_____ZONE THERAPY: A Guide to Applied-Pressure Therapy by Anika Bergson & Vladimir Tuchack   P456 $1.25

_____FOOD TO IMPROVE YOUR HEALTH: A Complete Guide to Over 300 Foods for 101 Common Ailments by Linda Pelstring & Jo Ann Hauck   P637 $1.50

_____HOW TO HELP YOUR DOCTOR HELP YOU by Jessyca Russell Gaver   P587 $1.75

_____RELAXERCISES: Remodel Yourself the Rhythmic Way by Joan Fraser. Fully illustrated   P088 $1.25

_____BODYMIND: The Whole Person Health Book by Don Ethan Miller   P566 $1.50

_____PSYCHOSOMATICS: How Your Emotions Can Damage Your Health by Howard R. and Martha E. Lewis   P532 $1.75

and a top bestseller:

_____THE THIN BOOK, By a Formerly Fat Psychiatrist, Theodore Isaac Rubin, M.D.
                       P777 $1.25

Check which books you want. If you can't find any of these books at your local bookstore, simply send cover price plus 25¢ per book for postage and handling to:
PINNACLE BOOKS,
275 Madison Avenue, New York, N.Y. 10016